Memoirs of Captain Sam Bellamy, The Prince of Pirates: Saint Croix, 1716-1717

John A. Boyd

Copyright 2015 John A. Boyd

Published By:

Create Space Independent Publishing Platform Charleston SC

Memoirs of Captain Sam Bellamy, the Prince of Pirates: Saint Croix, 1716-1717

ISBN-13. 978-1517768058 (CreateSpace-Assigned)
ISBN-10: 1517768055
LCCN:
BISAC: History / Caribbean & West Indies / General

Other books by John Boyd:

Caribs: The Original Caribbean Pirates & Founding Fathers of American Democracy (2013)

ISBN-13: 978-1482627138 (CreateSpace-Assigned)
ISBN-10: 1482627132
LCCN: 2013906486
BISAC: History / Native American

The Lost Pirate Treasure of St. Croix: Your Search for Billions Start Here (2013)

ISBN-13: 978-1490536392 (CreateSpace-Assigned)
ISBN-10: 1490536396
LCCN: 2013912438
BISAC: History / Caribbean & West Indies / General

Dedication

To all those who encourage my story telling whether they believe me or not.

To my daughter, Dagny, who warns people never to bet against the truth of my tall tales. She also encourages me to focus on the task at hand and finish my projects one by one.

To Crab Claw Willy who did a fact check on my book on the Lost Pirate Treasures of St. Croix and found a single error where I had transposed two numbers in a date. As a historian, Crab Claw Willy has encouraged me to write more stories. As a scoundrel, he has warned that if I do not, he will steal them as his own. As a poet, he uses the stories as inspirations for the songs he writes.

Table of Contents

Prologue 1
   Reflections on Olivier Levasseur 1
Chapter 1 18
   Early Childhood 18
Chapter 2 27
   Merchant City of Exeter 27
Chapter 3 39
   Life in the Royal Navy 39
Chapter 4 57
   Sam Bellamy Falls in Love 57
Chapter 5 70
   Sam Plans to be a Treasure Hunter 70
Chapter 6 78
   A Rough Start to a Good Plan! 78
Chapter 7 93
   Mysteries of the Serranilla Banks 93
Chapter 8 104
   An Accidental Pirate 104
Chapter 9 125
   Water, Fuel, Meat, Provisions and Fruit 125
Chapter 10 131
   People to Work the Land 131
Chapter 11 137
   Surrounded by a Few Good Men & then there were none 137
Chapter 12 151
   Gambling on His Future! 151
Chapter 13 157
   A New Ship for the New Adventure. 157
Chapter 14 165
   Poseidon's Revenge! 165
Chapter 15 174
   Final Reflections From St. Croix 174
Aftermath 185
   After the Whydah Wreck. 185
Epilogue 193
   Are the Memoirs True? 193
Annotated Bibliography 201

List of Images

Prologue: Map of Malta in the 16th century, when Italian was declared the official language by the Knights of Malta. This image is in the public domain.

Chapter 1: Spectral hounds, Sidney Paget's illustration of The Hound of the Baskervilles. The story was inspired by a legend of ghostly black dogs in Dartmoor. Image is in the public domain; author died more than 70 years ago.

Chapter 2: John Rocque's 1744 map of Exeter. The copyright is in the public domain because it has expired.

Chapter 3: A period map marked with the site of the 1711 Quebec Expedition naval disaster. Herman Moll (1654–1732) This image is in the public domain.

Chapter 4: "The Sailor's Return" by Francis Wheatley, 1786, National Maritime Museum. This image is in the public domain.

Chapter 5: Portrait of Sir William Phips, first royal governor of the Province of Massachusetts Bay. This image is in the public domain.

Chapter 6: Serrana Banks, Copyright John Boyd

Chapter 7: Serranilla Banks, Copyright John Boyd

Chapter 8: Engraving depicting William Phips loading treasure found in a shipwreck in 1687. This image is in the public domain.

Chapter 9: Père Jean-Baptiste Labat, Front cover for "Nouveau Voyage aux Isles de l'Amerique by Jean-Baptiste Vol.1 (1722)." This image is in the public domain.

Chapter 10: Cannon Placement on 1671 Map of La Bassin. This image is in the public domain.

Chapter 11: Nineteenth century painting of vessels being careened by Louis Le Breton. This image is in the public domain.

Chapter 12: James Martel as depicted in "A General History of Pirates" by Captain Johnson. This image is in the public domain.

Chapter 13: Eighteenth century Map based on stolen Spanish information. "Insulae Americanae nempe Cuba, Hispaniola, Iamaica, Pto Rico, Lucania, Antillae vulgo Caribae, Barlo-et Sotto-Vento etc." This image is in the public domain.

Chapter 14: Poseidon holding a trident. Corinthian plaque, 550–525 BC. From Penteskouphia. This image is in the public domain.

Chapter 15: This map of Cape Cod is from a book by Capt. Cyprian Southack entitled, "The New England Coasting Pilot from Sandy Point of New York, unto Cape Canso in Nova Scotia, and Part of Island Breton. With the Courses and Distances from Place to Place, and towns on the Sea-Board; Harbours, Bays, Islands, Roads, Rocks, Sands: The Setting and Flowing of tides and Currents; with several other Directions of great Advantage to this Part of Navigation in North-America. By Capt. Cyprian Southack who has been Cruzing in the Service of the Crown of Great Britain Twenty-two years. The image from this book is in the public domain. **Note** there is an "X" just off the eastern shore of Wellfleet and to to the west of Crab Bank

Aftermath: A sketch of Sir Edmond Halley's Diving Bell for J. Hinton at the King's Arms on Newgate Street. This image is in the public domain.

Epilogue: Table listing the Slave-Trading Voyages of Captain Lawrence Prince (1709-1720). Also included are two more voyages (1721 & 1722) by Captain John Dagge in ships named Whidah owned by Humpry Morice. Source: *"Trans-Atlantic Slave Trade Database"* by Emory University.

Author's Introduction

This is a story about three pirate captains who worked together during the Golden Age of Piracy. The tale of Captain Paulsgrave Williams is a shared story with that of Captain Samuel Bellamy and is largely covered in this book. Their partner in crime, Olivier Levasseur, was perhaps the most successful pirate in the Golden Age of Piracy if the estimate of his wealth includes all of his Caribbean and African exploits.

Despite their partnership, Levasseur and Williams never made the Forbes' list of the Richest Caribbean Pirates while Bellamy did. The reason of course is simple. Sam Bellamy's ship, the Whydah, was wrecked and the vast amount of wealth carried on the ship was documented at trials of the survivors. There is little documentation of the wealth accumulated by Levasseur and there is no surviving estimate of the wealth that Williams earned.

After the Whydah sunk, Williams received the King's Pardon. He allegedly returned to piracy as a partner with Levasseur before disappearing from the public record. Levasseur was eventually hung after he retired from a life of Piracy when his negotiations with the King of France broke down. It seems he was richer than the King who wanted all his accumulated wealth in exchange for a pardon. Levasseur ended up hung and the King got nothing.

Before 1986, Sam Bellamy was hardly recognized by anyone outside of New England despite being credited as the most successful pirate of the Caribbean. He is believed to have died in a nor'easter on his way to reunite with his true love. Barry Clifford rediscovered the wreck and has been promoting Captain Bellamy and the Whydah Gally ever since.

I am fortunate to have had access to a manuscript allegedly written by Sam Bellamy himself. On St. Croix, there are several old families who can trace their roots back to the Knights of Malta and the English squatters who occupied St Croix after the French abandoned the island in 1696. One pirate who retired to become a planter was entrusted with the manuscript by Bellamy who decided to go to Cape Cod and reunite with his girlfriend before returning with her to St. Croix to start a planter's life.

My source could have just as easily been written by someone who knew Sam in St. Croix or a descendant of the planter who wanted to pass the story of a good man on to his children. Sam Bellamy's life makes a good story in an era when story telling and books were the only entertainment. The story is pretty much seditious and if made public at the time would have been a crime.

As the story of the manuscript is told, Sam took his wealth with him but left his personal possessions including his memoirs with the pirate turned planter. While not as detailed as the "Memoires of the Navy" by Samuel Pepys published in 1691, Sam's memoirs offer us glimpses of his childhood and the influences which led him to a life at sea as a pirate.

I got access to the manuscript with several conditions. I had to promise to never divulge my source. I could not remove, copy or photograph the manuscript. I was only allowed to carefully read the text for a few hours a day and make notes on the content. This made it a slow and tedious process as reading early 18th century script is difficult for me.

Because of the restrictions placed on me, I just tried to extract Sam's thoughts and report them in my own words. Also, I use the modern geographical descriptions to make it easier for the reader to follow Sam's movement in England during his formative years. For example, the river Yew is now called the Yeo; Ste. Croix is now St. Croix.

Our story starts with a description of Sam's early life and his journey from a very small village to a life at sea and his decision to move to America to seek his fortune. Sam mentioned his love affair with Maria Hallett as the reason he refocused his determination to pursue his fortune. He wanted to be wealthy so that he could overcome her parents' objections to his lowly status and marry the girl of his dreams.

Sam Bellamy rose from a sailor in the British Navy to become the Prince of Pirates and one of the Richest Caribbean Pirates ever. The other very rich pirate on the short list of those who might have taken more than one hundred million dollars was Olivier Levasseur, his co-regent in the St. Croix Pirate Republic.

There were many considerations in making St. Croix their base camp. The agriculture wealth of the island of St. Croix made it the perfect place to acquire firewood, meat, poultry, fish, provisions and water. There was also an agricultural community of illegal squatters to farm the land in exchange for trade goods and protection.

The pirates were able to transform the natural harbor around Bassin (Christensted) into an impenetrable military encampment and live peacefully and securely while on land.

For Sam Bellamy, the motivation for piracy was both his personal love for Maria Hallett and his desire for social justice and equality in his world. While social justice and equality were never achieved in his lifetime, his radical beliefs helped form the Republic called the United States of America.

John Boyd

November 13, 2015

Judith's Hill, St. Croix, U. S. Virgin Islands

Acknowledgment

I have to give tribute to my army of proofreaders who want little more than to improve my writing and make me a better person. They may win on the former but as to the latter, i am probably hopeless. I offer my sincere thanks to the following important people in my life who dramatically improved this work. Any mistakes or omissions are mine. In alphabetical order, my sincere thanks to:
Dagny Evans
Chuck Fischer
Melissa Smith
Jerlyn Thomas

Sixteenth Century Map of Malta,
Home of the Knights of Malta

Prologue

Reflections on Olivier Levasseur

Sam caught up with the French pirate La Buse for the second time while Captain Hornigold was away. They cruised the waters in the vicinity of Hispaniola in the month of June 1716 looking for ships of any nation. Since Paulsgrave Williams was now proficient at handling the Newport sloop, Sam got to spend a fair amount of time with Captain Olivier Levasseur.

Sam thanked Olivier for his previous help and the advice on how to protect his ship from pirates while continuing his wrecking operation to the southwest of Jamaica. He once again was asking for a huge favor as he needed a ship that could be converted to a man o' war to carry his wrecking fortune back to Boston without fear of pirate or navy ships stopping him. Sam proposed working together. Olivier could keep his share of the pirate treasure they took until Sam found his ship. All Sam wanted out of their agreement was a suitable ship. In principle, they agreed and spent time getting to know each other.

While cruising for victims, Sam questioned Olivier about his relation to Francois Levasseur, the first governor of the Pirate republic of Tortuga who was a naval officer and Huguenot. Olivier explained that French history was complex and not always logical so he had to listen carefully and try to understand. He would explain everything to him about his background, how he became a pirate and why he was comfortable with himself and his occupation.

However, if he was to spend his time giving Sam the best Naval education in the world, Sam would have to prove he was worthy of his help. He would give Sam an opportunity to think about the influences in his life that brought him to becoming a very wealthy pirate with hardly any pirating skills and try to convince Olivier that he was worthy of his continued help.

As a start to his education, Olivier explained that there were no Huguenots left in France. This group from the Northern part of France were Calvinists and were continuously persecuted by the Catholics of France. Francois Levasseur, a Huguenot, had risen through the ranks of the French Navy during a very unusual era of religious tolerance.

After 1610, conditions for Huguenots steadily declined. Around 1620, only Catholic officers were allowed in the Kings Navy so officers were recruited from French members of the Knights of Malta to take command of the largely protestant enlisted soldiers and sailors. This method seemed to work until King Louis XIV decided to eliminate all Protestants from France by any means necessary. His revocation of the Edict of Nantes in 1685 led to the deterioration of his military and political dominance. On 17 January 1686, Louis XIV himself claimed that out of a Huguenot population of 800,000 to 900,000 at the start of his reign, only 1,000 to 1,500 remained in France. In the future only Catholics could become soldiers and sailors and die for France.

Olivier's family was from Ile-de-Fance near Paris and were Catholic. They were peers from the Ile-de-France and held family seats in honor of Neuilly and Sailly. Peers were considered untitled nobility but still entitled to seats in the Parliament of Paris which was the most important judicial court in the kingdom in close contact with the King.

Olivier was a little ashamed to admit that his family had benefited from the exodus of the Huguenots. At the start of the seventeenth century, his family were bourgeois landholders. They specialized in renting to merchants in the outskirts of Paris and, according to the desires of Henry IV, did not discriminate so their tenants included Dutch and French Protestants. Catholics at the time did not generally deal in commerce so all of their tenants were non-Catholic.

As pressure was put on Huguenots to convert or leave France many decided to close shop and leave. They offered their businesses to the Levasseur family to settle debts and in lieu of rent. His family made the decision to deal fairly with everyone. They would even legally help Huguenot businessmen who had converted to Catholicism get back in business. They reinvested their additional profits in new businesses and more land in Ile-de-France. As the family got more wealthy, they were hard for the king to ignore and were named Peers a couple of generations before Oliver was born.

As a second son born in 1683, Olivier was not entitled to inherit lands or a title but his father had a plan. He hired a priest to be in charge of his education with a total focus on military history and the priesthood. The goal was for him to join the Knights of Malta and become an officer in the French Military which might further the social standing of his family with both King and Country.

Olivier was close to the perfect student in training for the Knights of Malta. He believed absolutely everything his mother and the priests were teaching him about his Catholic faith. When there was a debate on an issue within the church he gravitated to the more conservative position. He avoided all sins, both mortal and venial [lessor]. While he was still too young for many of the seven deadly sins, he still avoided overeating or indulging in too much dinner or communion wine and learned to control his temper.

In the area of Military Science, he was almost the opposite. He studied historic battles and tactics and tried to improve them. He played chess to improve his tactical skills. He became so good his father hired a professional chess player to challenge him. Military Science gave him the freedom of expression he denied himself in his religious studies.

At age 12, he was deemed ready by his tutors to join the Knights of Malta and he was rated excellent in all his interviews prior to joining the order. Olivier thought the decision was entirely his own based on his life long education. The only problem standing in his way was that his family's claim to nobility was neither strong nor long. It is true that they had been peers for a couple of generations but they had no specific title and generally four generations or 100 years was considered old nobility. King Louis XIV interceded on behalf of Olivier in exchange for family support on a few issues in the Parliament of Paris and a larger than normal donation to the Knights from the family in the name of the king.

The first four years at Malta held no surprises. He attended classes and mass each day and prayed for guidance. As Olivier gained in knowledge he continued to gain in both piety and tolerance for sinners who needed guidance.

As taught in his history classes, the Knights were originally created to provide medical care for pilgrims and crusaders traveling in the Holy Land. In time this function was expanded to a military function to protect pilgrims from attacks along the way. The Knights of Malta initially operated from Jerusalem but expanded to operate from a fort in the Kingdom of Cyprus to protect pilgrims on the sea route to the Holy Land. In 1210, they built a naval fleet manned by warrior Knights to police the Eastern Mediterranean.

In 1291, the massive manpower of the Ottoman Empire fighting on their own lands forced all of the Crusaders from the European Kingdom of Jerusalem. The Knights of Malta consolidated on the Island of Cyprus and continued to protect Catholic pilgrims in the Levant but never considered the Kingdom of Cyprus a permanent home.

The solution was for the knights to acquire by battle the Island of Rhodes from an Islamic ruler of the Byzantine Empire and establish their own separate state under the control of a Prince of the Church. At this time the Knights of Rhodes became a militant order dedicated to the defense of the Christian Faith. This required an expensive fortress on Rhodes and a naval force to protect Catholic shipping. After 1310, the Order built a powerful fleet and sailed the Eastern Mediterranean, fighting many famous battles.

The order had created a very expensive mission for their small country. They had to provide for their own national defense and police the known world against all enemies of the faith. For the first two centuries, they earned their revenues though the spoils of war and direct contributions from the Catholic Kingdoms of Europe, which was pretty much all of them.

Ultimately the power of the Knights of Rhodes and their disruption of shipping was too much for the Muslim world to ignore. The Knights withstood two invasions; one by the Sultan of Egypt in 1444 and another by the Ottoman Sultan, Mehmed II, in 1480. Finally in 1522, Sultan Suleiman the Magnificent arrived with 100,000 men in 400 ships. The 7000 Knights held out for six months before surrendering and being allowed to leave the island.

The Knights were homeless for eight years until the King of Spain who was also ruler of Malta and Sicily provided a solution. He would assign Malta as a permanent fiefdom of the order so long as they provided recognition to the King of Spain by delivering one Maltese Falcon each year to the Viceroy of Sicily.

After the move to Malta, the Knights immediately started to fortify the island recognizing that a return to their unbeatable Naval strength would mean a renewed attack by the Ottoman Empire. While fortifying their island home. the knights also started a Naval college that was acclaimed to be the best in the world. The orthodox history as taught in the monastery ignored the perspectives of Muslims, Jews and Protestants.

As taught, the Knights of Malta were the defenders of the Catholic Faith living off the generosity of the Catholic Kings of the Holy Roman Empire and whatever spoils of war they could capture from Infidel shipping in the Mediterranean (including Protestant and Jewish). They also attacked the port cities of the infidels and sacked them to recover Christians used as servants and Galley slaves. Of course, they recovered the ill-gotten gains of the infidels and claimed it as a prize of war to support the good deeds and military protection of all of Christendom in which the Knights were engaged.

The Knights of Malta were so successful at policing the Mediterranean that they once again came to the attention of Sultan Suleiman the Magnificent who had so generously let the surviving Knights leave Rhodes on Christmas Eve in 1522. By the early 1560's, he became convinced that he must destroy the order once and for all.

The Knights were prepared for the inevitable. They elected a warrior for their new Grand Master in 1557. The Knights elected Jean Parisot de Valette Grand Master of the Order. He was a naval commander for the order who continued his raids on non-Christian shipping. His private vessels are known to have taken 3,000 Muslim and Jewish slaves during his time as Grand Master. Also contributing to Suleiman's anger was another Knight Romegas, who in 1564, captured several large merchantmen including one that belonged to the Chief Eunuch of the the women's apartments in Suleiman's Palace. He also captured the governor of Cairo, the governor of Alexandria, and the former nurse of Suleiman's daughter. All were held for ransom.

The Great Siege of Malta started in the summer of 1565. Suleiman sent an armada of 193 ships and 36,000 fighting men against a defensive force of only 6000 men in arms on an island of 122 square miles. Suleiman's forces fired a total of 130,000 cannon balls at the island and the siege lasted for four hot summer months. By the time Christian reinforcements arrived from Italy, the invasion forces had already started retreating and the Knights had won. Malta had lost one third of the defenders (2000 men) and the Ottoman Empire lost about the same percentage (12,000 men.)

After this victory, the Christian Rulers of Europe all provided support for the Knights of Malta to be the first line of defense against the Ottoman Empire. The new revenues allowed the Knights to build the most advanced Hospitals, medical schools and Universities in all of Europe. Malta was transformed from a poor barren island to one of the most attractive cities of Europe. The Naval Academy became the most advanced in the world.

Discipline at the Academy was strict and exacting. The Order became a training ground for European royal navies, particularly France and Spain. The Knight's navy attracted other naval officers including Swedes and Russians, who were not affiliated with the Order as were the French and Spanish Knights, but who volunteered to serve for two or three years in the Order's navy to learn the techniques of sea warfare. Some of their naval campaigns against the Ottoman Empire, called Caravans, lasted that long. The raids by the knights and their galleys were so frequent and powerful that authorities from the Ottoman Empire were wondering if Malta was more powerful than France.

During his four years in the Seminary, Olivier had excelled in the Military and Naval History of Malta. At age 16, he became a priest in the order of Malta and was faced with a decision. If he wanted to remain a priest in service to the order, there were no further requirements. However, if he wanted to be a full-fledged Knight of Malta, he would have to spend a year in a Maltese Galley defending Christians from the terrors of the Ottoman Empire in the Mediterranean Sea. He was determined to put his knowledge of military tactics to use and joined the next available galley. Up to this point he believed all he had been taught.

Olivier was delivered to the dock just before his ship sailed, but Olivier was still shocked by a phenomenon he didn't yet understand. On the dock were women and children crying and waving at the Knights that were going to sea to battle the Ottoman Empire. Once they got to sea, everything seemed normal and Olivier forgot about the emotional departure. As the newest member, Olivier was a marine and part of the boarding party.

In his youthful exuberance to be of value to his Order and his God, he attacked his opponents with speed and determination. He sought out the professional Warrior on an Infidel ship who enjoyed his job because he was sick at heart due to his lack of faith in God. If he could kill the leader, the battle for the ship would end. Like a buzzard, he would jump from a perch on his ship to the deck of the victim's ship plummeting downward in a spiral, twisting and turning with his sword in motion towards any enemy he saw, finally reaching his intended target who he ruthlessly dispatched. His bravery was noted by his shipmates who started calling him La Buse, The Buzzard, but not disrespectfully.

His first tour of duty at sea was typical. They went to the Barbary Coast and engaged a few Barbary pirates. They took the treasure and provisions that were on their ships and freed the Christian Galley slaves. They also enslaved the Islamic and Moorish sailors whether free or slave. When they had a sufficient number of additional Christians, they joined forces with other Maltese galleys in the area. The fleet sacked coastal towns with the intent of freeing additional Christians but all they seemed to accomplish was the looting of the towns for anything of value as there were no other Christian slaves in town. At this time most of the Galleys had had a very successful voyage and they returned as a fleet to Malta after a fairly typical three-year Caravan.

Upon arrival, the Captain took Olivier aside and explained that each Knight on the Caravan was entitled to a share of the prize money captured from the Galley including the money gained by selling the slaves. Because the Order was now financially dependent on the privateering activities of the Maltese Navy, the Knights of the Navy were allowed to spend the money any way they wanted and their transgressions would be forgiven. They could engage in sins of the flesh in the coastal towns, save for a ship of their own or find a wife and have a family and children. All would be forgiven so long as they were successful at providing the funds the order needed to survive and support their Hospitals and Universities.

A very perplexed Olivier sought out his Priest Confessor to gain a greater understanding of what had happened to his Order and how he should respond as a righteous man in the eyes of God. The Confessor explained that after the Great Siege of Malta, there had been an unprecedented flow of funds from the Catholic Princes and Kings and the Emperor of the Holy Roman Empire. This allowed the order to increase their defenses, build new cities, create hospitals and build new universities.

The island became a center of Art and Culture for all of Europe. The navy became the most powerful in the Mediterranean. However, before they could complete all that they had started, the Holy Roman Empire and all of the Catholic Monarchs of Europe began to self-destruct in wars of moral conscience and petty jealousy. France and Spain were in a constant state of War starting in 1521 and even the gift of Malta to the Order was more likely a political gesture than a religious one.

Starting in 1525 when the French were at a disadvantage because Spain had imprisoned Francis I, King of France, French officials started making overtures to the Ottoman Empire and from 1530 to 1559, Spain was in a constant state of War in Hungary and Italy with an Alliance of France and the Ottoman Empire opposing Spain. Since many of the Knights were French, the Order provided a safe harbor that the Ottoman's were unlikely to attack and thus Spain would have one less worry in their war against France. The presence of the Knights of Malta served France equally as well. In 1536, France negotiated a trade agreement with the Ottoman Empire.

At the time trade between Europe and the Levant was pretty much the domain of the Sephardic Jews expelled from Spain and their Merchant Network. They worked closely with the Muslim Traders in terms of financing and insuring the merchandise against loss at sea. They also traveled on the Muslim ships to protect their investment. By attacking the merchant ships at sea, the Knights got Muslim and Moorish slaves and Jews who were held for ransom in addition to all the treasure the merchant ships contained. This was far easier and more profitable work then pursuing the Barbary pirates. Of course this effort was ignored or sanctioned by both France and Spain. French merchants had weaker competition and Spain still officially persecuted Jews and Muslims.

The only sustained peace in that era was from 1559 until 1568. Suleiman's spies told him that both France and Spain were momentarily tired of War and were unlikely to provide military support to Malta so he began his siege of Malta in 1565. Unfortunately, luck and determination were on the side of the Knights of Malta and they survived the siege.

For a very short while, the Knights received generous financial support from the Catholic Kingdoms of Europe but France and Spain went to war again in 1568 and various wars occupied them for the next 100 years. The Knights were on their own to pay their bills. It was during this era that Warrior Knights were rewarded and encouraged to engage in any activity to increase privateering revenues to the Order. This eventually led to the moral decline of the warrior Knights who engaged in marriages, families or just plain debauchery and the pursuit of additional wealth by becoming mercenaries in foreign Navies.

After talking with his Confessor, Olivier resolved his problem in a manner that would leave his morals unblemished and still allow him to serve his Order to the best of his ability. He decided to remain in the Maltese Navy and give every bit of his prize money to the Order to continue the good works they had started over one hundred years earlier. Trying to eliminate the Barbary Coast Pirates was a good objective and if money was recovered while they freed the Christian Galley slaves and killed all pirates, so much the better.

Olivier did one more tour of duty to the Barbary Coast and was satisfied with his successes and position in life and once again gave his share of the prize money to the Knights of Malta to continue their good deeds. On his second caravan, he still led the raiding party of young Knights, but also, spent far more time learning to become a sailor and a future captain of a galley.

Oliver's next assignment was his most educational and lucrative. He was assigned to be Captain of a galley that was to search out and capture rich merchant ships. This duty usually went to older, more seasoned Captains who owned their own ships. Olivier was to be in charge of one of the Galleys owned by the Order and, to maximize their revenues, they assigned Olivier to this ship.

The older Captains with their own ships usually had families at home and no longer wanted to take great risks taking the best Merchantmen. There were no longer captains like Valette and Romegas had been in 1564 and it was only the slowest, oldest and poorest ships that were being captured by these great caravans against Ottoman shipping. This was unfortunate because the fleet of Galleys needed supply ships and transport ships to continuously bring supplies to the Captains and return to Malta with slaves, hostages and treasure. The Port Captain thought he could increase the recovered wealth by putting an aggressive person like Olivier in the fleet as captain of his own galley with freedom to rove the open sea in search of prey.

The first two-year caravan was a total success for Oliver. He would maneuver his ship to approach the merchant ship from the direction the wind was pushing the merchantman. Thus, he would slow the merchant ship from loss of wind and swoop down from its most indefensible stern angle. He would loot the ship and skip taking hostages. In that manner he could avoid feeding hostages and avoid contact with the transport and supply ships. He got all the supplies he needed from the merchant ships he intercepted.

When he returned to Malta, everybody was amazed at the amount of wealth he accumulated and also by the total lack of slaves and hostages. Malta was accustomed to the ransom on Jews and the sale of slaves being just as valuable as the trade goods and money captured while privateering. No one in the port recognized that he had taken more than twice as many ships and accumulated much more wealth than other captains because he was not slowed down by the human cargo. All they seemed to dwell on was how much richer he would be if he took it all.

While on shore, Oliver directed a letter to his family. Another European war had started and France and Spain were on the same side. He knew the Order would release him for fear of offending the King so he wanted his family to secure a Letter of Marque from the King and acquire a ship for him to be a privateer working for France. In this war, the targets would be the rich European countries like England, Holland and Portugal. Morally, he would avoid fighting his fellow Catholics and make war against the Protestant Nations. Before he got a response, it was time to go to war again against the rich merchant ships of the Mediterranean.

This time the same captains who had ignored him in the last campaign were now stalking him. Once he stopped a ship, they took turns being part of the boarding party gaining a share of the wealth, hostages and slaves of the ship. As a moral Frenchman, Oliver was against enslaving any people as there were no slaves in France and no slave markets. He did not do it so he turned his head in the other direction when the other Captains did it for "the good of the Order". His dilemma in holding the Muslim merchants and ships captain along with the Jewish financiers was even worse. Many spoke French and some of the Jews had families who had lived in France prior to being expelled. All of these people had their own faith, all believed in the Prophets of the Old Testament and many lived more exemplary lives than his fellow Knights of Malta working as privateers.

Olivier returned to Malta a changed man. He still had his faith in God and his religion. However, he had lost all faith in the men who compromised their values in the name of God and the Order of the Knights of Malta. He also recognized that others of different religions had just as much faith in God as he had and the differences were not worth fighting over unless you were attacked. He got his Letter of Marque just in time to avoid expressing any negative views within the Order and went off to France to get his ship and crew and serve his King. In this case he knew that this was a political war and he would serve his king best by making as much money as possible fighting all of those who had been born in a country other than France or Spain. He smiled when he thought that it was almost a Calvinist belief that God would judge his merit to go to heaven by the amount of wealth he acquired and not necessarily by his good deeds.

Sam Bellamy found a kindred spirit in Olivier Levasseur. He too still maintained his belief in God but had lost all faith in a minister's ability to interpret the word of God or provide meaningful guidance to parishioners. He went one step further than Olivier. He had no faith in his King to provide leadership to his people that would benefit anybody except the King.

Sam had a lot to think about if he were to share his important life's experiences with Olivier. It was time to organize his thoughts so he started his memoirs.

Sam Bellamy would eventually learn about piracy from perhaps the Greatest Pirate of the Golden Age of piracy. Olivier Levasseur was the French pirate, nicknamed La Buse, French for the Buzzard, because of the speed and ruthlessness that he used when a young privateer operating in the Mediterranean and attacking the ships of the Ottoman Empire. He had studied in the Maltese Naval Academy for four years and honed his skills as a privateer in the Mediterranean for seven more years.

Spectral Hound of Dartmoor

Chapter 1
Early Childhood

Sam Bellamy was the youngest of six children, born in 1689, to Steffen and Elizabeth Bellamy in the village of Hittisleigh in Devonshire, England. His mother died in childbirth and was buried on February 23, 1689, three weeks before Samuel's baptism on March 18. The church was just a short walk down the street from the Bellamy home.

Sam was born to a loving Christian family of five older siblings who contributed positively to his upbring and education. His oldest brother, Harry. was 12 when he was born. Harry was very close to the two oldest girls, Elizabeth (age 8) and Rose (age 10), who buried their grief by lovingly caring for their new baby brother who was all alone in the world.

It wasn't very long before Steffen took a second wife, Betsy, to help raise his family. Betsy had been a spinster all her life and was a wife of convenience to help Steffen raise his brood. She was so good natured that the family grew to love her, especially the two younger children Robert age five and Joan age two, who were largely ignored after the birth of Samuel and the death of their mother.

Sam, as he was called from a very early age, was an outgoing, intelligent and very curious young man who wanted to know everything. He was comfortable talking, discussing and even arguing with people beyond his age and asking questions of strangers he would meet. Since his father and older brother were away from home all day working as farmers and day laborers, Sam was often left alone to wander in the village as his sisters shooed him away so they could do their chores.

The local Anglican minister, Reverend Robert, and his wife took a liking to Sam. The Church of St. Andrew was on Eastchurch Lane just a short walk from Sam's house. The minister envisioned the intelligent, charismatic boy to be a future alter boy and started to teach him to read and write at an early age.

For over six months a year, the temperature on the moor was between freezing and the mid forties [Fahrenheit] with an average of 7.2 inches of rain, snow, sleet and hail during those months. Sam had no problems staying inside the warm house of Reverend Robert and getting fed while studying. He was an exceptional student enjoying what he thought was a very good life.

About the time Sam was six, he started exploring the moor around his house. He soon found that there were several streams within 1000 feet of Hittisleigh and the Yeo River was less than a mile away. On the few hot summer days each year, Sam would enter the very cold, rapidly moving water of the nearby streams and after getting swept away a few times, he learned to enjoy swimming. Because of the wicked currents of the river Yeo and the surrounding streams, Sam eventually became a powerful, fearless swimmer.

Hittisleigh was in England's moor region, which is the highlands with high rainfall zones. The area around Hittisleigh was divided by streams and rivers as the excessive rain water ran to the sea. Homes on the moors were made of natural granite in the style of a longhouse with a single room and the Bellamy clan lived in a sturdy longhouse.

Most of the time Sam spent studying with Reverend

Robert focused on reading the Bible although Sam was also taught Latin and enough simple math to run a household or a village church. He also had access to several books in the priest's library. The library included some of Shakespeare's plays along with "Memoires of the Navy" by Samuel Pepys published in 1691.

Sam was fond of the book by Samuel Pepys who was an English naval administrator and Member of Parliament. It was not the book which attracted Sam as much as it was the author's personal history. His father, John Pepys, was a tailor and his mother, Margaret Pepys, was the daughter of a Whitechapel butcher. With education, hard work, and his talent for administration, Pepys rose to be the Chief Secretary of the Admiralty under both King Charles II and King James II. His influence and reforms at the Admiralty were important in the development of a professional Royal Navy.

Sam became convinced that by hard work and education he could rise above his common birth and become a person of distinction just as Samuel Pepys had done.

Sam loved the Bible but was also impressed by the wisdom of William Shakespeare. His favorite life lesson from Shakespeare came from the play Julius Caesar, Act 2, Scene II, when Caesar says "Cowards die many times before their deaths; The valiant never taste of death but once." He reminded himself of this quote quite often as he explored his environment and developed his swimming skills.

As time passed, Sam became proficient at studying the moor and studying the King James version of the Holy Bible. This led to a moral conflict, which was to help form his lifetime beliefs and drive him from the Church of England. The conflict focused on the rights of royalty and the plight of the common man especially as it related to his right to walk in the estate called Dartmoor.

Sam first became attracted to Dartmoor because of the horror stories told about this forbidden place. Dartmoor was a royal forest area reserved by the king for hunting. In 1337, King Edward III granted the forest to Edward, the Black Prince, and at the same time made him the first Duke of Cornwall. Hunting, fishing or even trespassing were all strictly forbidden except by order of the King.

The prohibitions were enforced by a sheriff, but legends, folklore and myths warned of dire consequences for those who entered the forests. It was warned that Dartmoor was the haunt of a pack of "spectral hounds", a headless horseman, and an exceptionally large black dog who attacked all who entered the Duke's Forest, especially children.

Legend tells of the Devil's visit to the Dartmoor village of Widecombe-in-the-moor [Withy-combe], which caused the Great Thunderstorm of 1638. Dartmoor also had it's share of haunted places from restless spirits around graves and also other sites where people had experienced sudden deaths while crossing Dartmoor on their journeys or had an accident while hunting.

Sam had been hearing these tails from his father and oldest brother from the time he started walking around his village. When he first started exploring the countryside at age six, he took them to heart and only explored north of his house in the opposite direction of Dartmoor. He was afraid of Dartmoor and avoided the game preserve.

After learning to climb the granite outcroppings around his home and learning to swim in the rapidly moving streams, he decided he had to conquer the unknown fears of Dartmoor or remain a coward every time he was faced with ghost stories or other superstitions.

In the summer of his eleventh year, Sam started to explore the Yeo River and the outskirts of Dartmoor. He prayed to God for strength and protection and constantly repeated the 23rd Psalm to remind himself of his pledge to "fear no evil". He listened carefully for every sound and when he heard a rabbit, fox or deer running through the bush, he ran in fright out of the forest. Unlike most young boys he kept testing himself and returning to Dartmoor to learn it's secrets.

By the summer of his twelfth year, he had lost all fear and was exporting the incredible rock formations of Dartmoor. He knew that some formations were made by men and some by God, but he couldn't always tell who created them or for what purpose. He learned to love the lonely solitude of Dartmoor.

On his thirteenth birthday in 1702, Reverend Robert gave him a copy of "A New Voyage Round the World" by William Dampier. The book described global sailing trips to gain knowledge and wealth from the still unexplored new worlds from the Americas to Australia. Sam was also attracted to this book because of the social mobility of the author. William Dampier was the son of a tenant farmer, which was socially a step up from farmworkers like his family, but still considered commoners. Of course Sam intensified his studies and did whatever Reverend Robert requested.

With the start of the next summer Sam continued his

explorations of Dartmoor. There were legends of stone circles that occasionally had a man made small cave [crypt] in the center. These simple structures had four flat stones for the sides and a larger stone to cover the opening. The presences of bones and ashes indicated they were probably graves but locally they had many names indicating they could be a source of wealth including Roman graves, money pits, money boxes and crocks of gold.

Sam dreamed of finding enough gold so that his father and brother could move up to being tenant farmers and he could get the education he needed to become an officer in the Royal Navy. On his last trip, Sam got very excited when he found an unopened burial crypt. In his excitement, he stopped being wary of unusual sounds and diligently worked at opening the grave. Just as he achieved success, he was grabbed by the Sheriff of Dartmoor. The Sheriff seized the contents of the grave in the name of Queen Anne.

While the contents were nothing more than pottery, carved wood and beads, Sam thought he was the rightful owner because he found the cave and did the work to open it up and recover the almost worthless items. The Sheriff's two assistants held Sam while the Sheriff explained to Sam he was in serious trouble as he was trespassing on Queen Anne's private estate and trying to steal Royal possessions.

Sam was given the choice of trial and jail in London or volunteering to join the Duke of Cornwall's 32nd Regiment of Foot, which was an infantry regiment of the British Army. Sam used all his guile and logic to convince the Sheriff that he had no ill intentions and was diligently studying to become a Naval Officer. Sam knew that Army Officers were commissioned by the King for their nobility and not their ability. While an educated person had a chance of rising through the ranks in the Royal Navy, a foot soldier would never get promoted. If he were trapped in the Army he would more than likely end up dead in a war that would not benefit the common man.

The Sheriff turned him over to Father Robert and made him responsible for any future trespassing in Dartmoor which Sam promised not to do. However, Sam became very stubborn when Father Robert tried to explain to him the Divine Right of Kings and the obligations of commoners.

The Divine Right of Kings was a Christian political doctrine that hereditary monarchy is the system approved by God. The hereditary right cannot be forfeited or the power usurped by commoners.

The monarchs are only accountable to God for their actions, and rebellion against the lawful sovereign is therefore blasphemous. This belief was firmly entrenched in the 17th century and the only recourse for those who opposed it was to leave and go to the American colonies to avoid persecution as a Religious Dissenter. English supporters of Monarchy supported Divine Right in opposition to the more liberal religious theories of the Whigs and Puritans.

The doctrine embraced the belief that kings are the direct representatives of God, and as such are to receive the obedience due to God's viceroy on earth. They owe obedience to God alone, and are relieved from all responsibilities towards their subjects.

Sam argued vehemently with Father Robert and used the Old Testament prophet Samuel to support his point of view that God does not support the actions of Kings but actually disapproves of them. That was too much for Father Robert of the Church of

England and he accused Sam of blasphemy and ordered him to leave his house and the village of his birth and never return or he would notify the Sheriff of his seditious beliefs.

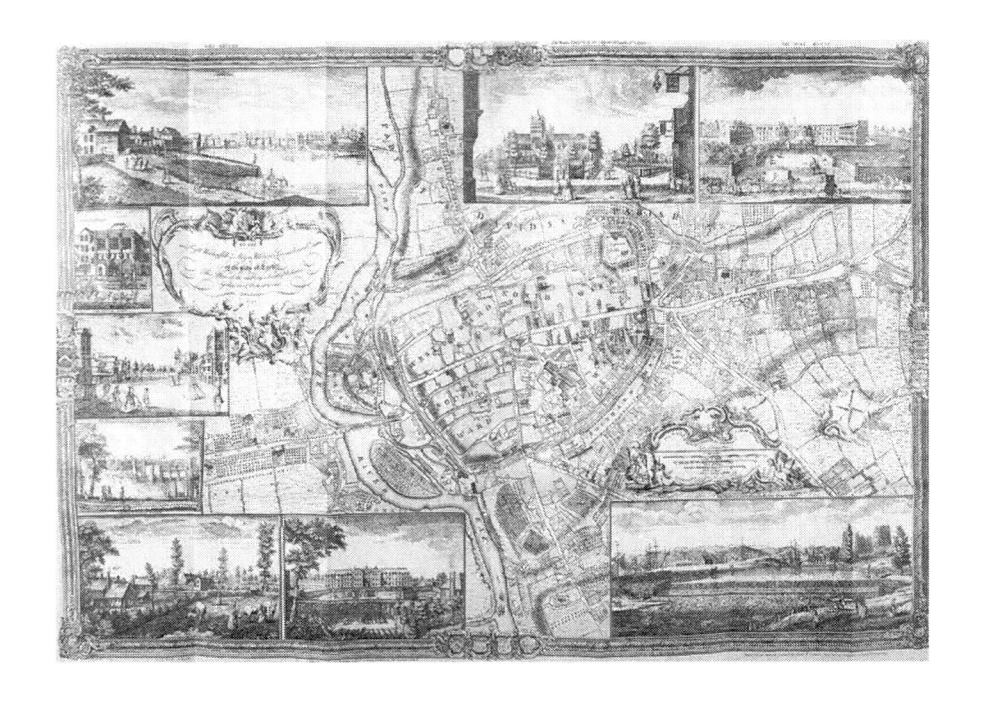

Eighteenth Century Port of Exeter

Chapter 2

Merchant City of Exeter

In the summer of his fourteenth year, Sam was forced to leave the village of Hittisleigh in Devonshire, England. In fact, Sam was not really sad. He had an easier childhood than most of his siblings and friends. Father Robert had fed him, clothed him and kept him warm in winter.

His family had also benefited from the patronage and work Father Robert had directed towards his family. Everyone in his family urged him to stop exploring the Royal Forests, repent his sins of pride and blasphemy and beg forgiveness from Father Robert so everything would remain the same and he could continue his education for the benefit of his whole family.

In reality Sam was ready to move on and conquer the world. He was a strong young man who embraced the cold torrential rivers and streams of Devonshire and he was ready to go to sea without fear of water, ghosts, pain or any other threat to his existence.

Before Sam left home he traded with his older brother for some work clothes as everything he owned and wore came from Father Robert and was more suitable for church meetings than for walking to Exeter or doing manual labor. His growth spurt over the past winter left him with a shortage of older clothes that he could wear when he was exploring and the Sheriff had caught him in early spring before he wore out any of his newer clothes.

When he left home, Sam had enough food for a day plus some of his new clothes. He had no problem finding work, especially as he got closer to Exeter. It seems that many boys and men had moved to the city for greater financial rewards and along the way Sam was only trying to exchange his labor for food and lodging.

One unexpected benefit was an excess of girls and young women left behind as the men moved to the city. Sam was flattered by all the attention he received from the young women and a couple of times he was tempted to stay and abandon his dreams of joining the Royal Navy. He constantly reminded himself that God had blessed him with the courage, intelligence, health, ability and education he would need to succeed in the Royal Navy so God wanted him to be a Sailor.

Sam followed the trails and paths along the River Yeo until it joined the River Creedy, which ends where it joins the River Exe at Cowley Bridge. The River Exe flows almost directly south and reaches the sea as a substantial river.

The river fueled Exeter's growth and relative importance in medieval times, and the city's first industrial area was developed on Exe Island, which was artificially created. The city waterfront had been constantly modified since the 13th century with areas of landfill and dredging creating islands where water wheels ran the textile industry weaving fabric from wool. There was even an engineering marvel built hundreds of years earlier which limited tidal interference in the bay which would have disrupted the water wheels yet still allowed the passage of ships.

Exeter was an economically powerful city with a strong trade of wool. This was partly due to the surrounding area which was very fertile with ample rain and water for the sheep. Sam found a city of over thirty thousand people employed as part of the wool and cloth industries. Merchandise was manufactured and sold to the West Indies, Spain, France and Italy. Town merchants bragged that international trade was so great the city generated more English wealth than any place in England including London.

When Sam reached Exeter, it seemed that almost every factory had help wanted signs so Sam took his time and wandered around talking to people. He went to the docks and found that while the Royal Navy was desperately recruiting sailors, Sam was too big and old for a boat boy and for other positions, the Navy wanted trained sailors of any nation.

The manning of ships was under the control of Prince George of Denmark who was Queen Anne's consort and Lord High Admiral. One of his duties was administering five ports on the Channel coast of England including Exeter. In his job, he chose porters, gunners and regimental officers, as well as settled squabbles about who runs what. He also regulated impressment of Danish fishermen to man the English Royal Navy ships.

Despite the fact that Sam wanted to join the Royal Navy, he did not have the necessary skills to be recruited or impressed.

Sam started to do odd jobs around the merchant ships and it wasn't long before one of the richer merchants recognized that he could read. At this point, Christopher Mitchell was to become the second most important person in Sam's future life. Sam still recognized all the good that Father Robert had done for him and was a little sorry that it didn't work out but Sam wanted to join the Royal Navy and make something of himself.

The merchant was fifteen years older than Sam, about the same age as his oldest brother. He had been born to a prosperous Leghorn Family and as they became friends, Christopher told Sam all about Leghorn and his Father's business which brought him to Exeter.

Leghorn was created when the "Livornine" laws and Constitution were established by the Grand Duke of Tuscany, Ferdinando I dé Medici about a century earlier [1593]. These laws made Leghorn [Livorno] a free-port and attracted a great number of merchants who were also granted freedom of religion and amnesty from prior debts and bankruptcies. The Constitution was designed to give sanctuary to Jews but it also sheltered merchants of all nations.

The port gained in popularity during times of war by remaining a neutral free port regardless of whether the wars were political, religious or economic. War was almost a constant state of affairs during the sixteenth and seventeenth centuries so Leghorn [Livorno], Italy, grew very prosperous.

The port and the city contained several dynamic foreign communities, organized in "Nations". Only the Jews were considered Tuscan subjects because they had no other sovereign state to defend them, or a place where they could be deported to, return to, or call home. English, Dutch, French, Greek, Armenian, Spanish, Portuguese, Sardinian, Swedish, Danish, Austrian, Prussian and others were represented by their consuls and governed by them to settle disputes. Each group had their own section with churches and cemeteries.

Sam was fifteen and Christopher was thirty when he

became Sam's mentor and surrogate big brother. They discussed everything from religion to war. Christopher did not approve of political, religious or economic wars but he did concede that merchant ships had to be protected against pirates and privateers. If there was no trade, the whole world would have a lower standard of living as England grew no spices and the Caribbean wove no fabric.

Samuel Mitchell of Leghorn and his son Christopher came to Exeter in 1677 and established Mitchell and Son. Christopher was only 3 years old at the time of the move. He grew up in Exeter so he knew all the merchants, captains and businessmen around the docks and was well connected. As a matter of trust, he helped Sam get work as a letter writer and courier by using his reputation to initially help his friend Sam get accepted.

When Christopher asked Sam about his religious beliefs, Sam explained he still believed in God but did not believe in the Church of England. Sam simply could not accept that an unjust monarch would be God's emissary on earth and capriciously rule over his subjects who had no say in matters.

Christopher explained that in matters of conscience, he was comfortable as both a Jew and a Christian. When he was in private, he engaged in all of his family's Jewish religious traditions. In Exeter, he considered himself a Christian of convenience going to any Christian Church he was invited to by merchants and ships captains.

His father had Baptized him in Leghorn in the Church of England and Christopher was the name given to him at Baptism. As a youth, he had attended the Church of England but as the nonconformists became more prominent as merchants and captains, he had no problem joining them in their services.

Christopher's father Samuel Mitchell was actually descended from a long line of Sephardic merchants who had been trading across the Mediterranean for centuries. He had been known in Leghorn, Italy, as Samuel Michon, whose family was part of a complex system of global trade based on religion, family ties and trust built up over decades and even generations.

They had close relatives in France and Turkey who were all part of the trading network despite the fact that France and England were at war. Samuel Michon had changed his family name to Mitchell because that was an old Scottish name and he wanted his son to blend in with the local populous as a Christian.

According to Christopher, pretty much all religions were trying to convince their followers to live a good life, do good deeds and worship one God. Christ was a Jew and followed the Jewish Law, and Christian churches accepted the Old Testament. Christopher urged Sam to start becoming a "Christian of convenience" and accept all invitations to attend church.

During times when Sam didn't get invited, Christopher urged him to just pick the church he liked best. As to the law of God, all faiths accepted the Ten Commandments so obey them, do good deeds and worship the one God of all the faiths. For, if there truly is only one God, he must be the same one for all the different religions.

Sam was not sure he understood everything that Christopher said about religion but he simplified his advice to a few rules; go to church every Sunday, obey the Ten Commandments and do good deeds that don't hurt yourself. One other piece of advice was to avoid any serious relationships with a woman until he was rich enough to afford a family.

The only connection of that rule to religion was that if he got a Christian girl pregnant, he would have to marry her and it would impact his ability to go to sea and continue working with captains and merchants. If he hung around with loose women he would be judged poorly and it would damage his reputation and ability to get work.

When he wanted the company of a woman, Sam could go to sea to a foreign port or take a trip to London. Sam was now being asked to deliver important letters to London and across the Channel to Amsterdam.

The business dealings of Mitchell and Son were extremely complex. The Sephardic Jews began to specialize in diamonds and jewels after they were expelled from most European Countries. While initially scattered to the Levant and the Americas, by the mid 1500's, they were allowed to settle in Italy and The Netherlands. The diamond cutters settled in Amsterdam. Raw diamonds were hard to dispose of unless you dealt with those skilled diamond cutters who were part of the trading network.

The market in Mediterranean Red Coral was controlled by Italian merchants. After being harvested, cut and polished, it was sold in Europe but could also be exchanged with Hindu Cast Members in Gao, India, for uncut diamonds. These diamonds were relatively worthless to the Italians but when delivered to the Italian Christian Merchants residing in Portugal, they could be passed on to Sephardic merchants in Holland for finishing and sales.

This complex network of international trade had members from several nations and varying religions, including Christians, Jews and Hindus, and was built up over generations based on reputation and trust. The only way a new member would be accepted was if a highly trusted member like Christopher Mitchell wrote a letter of introduction and pledged to be financially responsible for the person he recommended. It would take a generation of service before Sam would be trusted enough to recommend anyone and then only if he had established his reputation and fortune.

Portugal technically controlled Gao, and the Italians residing in Lisbon had good connections for supplying Red Coral to India and for disposing of the uncut diamonds. Whether the trade was legal or illegal, the diamonds were easily smuggled by friendly ship's Captains because the small packages of great value could be easily hid on board ships. When legal, small hidden packages were a safer way to transport valuables at sea and when illegal, it was the only possible way.

Several events happened which prompted Samuel Mitchell to move to Exeter. In 1650, England allowed the return of Jewish merchants. In 1664, Parliament eliminated any restrictions against the importation of uncut diamonds because they were impossible to regulate due to the small package size. When this happened, London became a merchant center for finished diamonds and uncut stones. The cutting was still done almost exclusively in Amsterdam.

Demand for red coral in India was greater than the supply of raw diamonds in India. The solution was for the Indian merchants to offer, and the Sephardic merchants to accept, that Indian cloth would be used to balance the trade deficit. Since Exeter was the trade center for English cloth, Samuel Mitchell became the agent for the Leghorn network distributing the Indian cloth to England and shipping the excess all over the world.

Eventually, Sam Bellamy was trusted to run a few courier assignments for the Merchants of Exeter carrying small valuable packages across the Channel to Amsterdam, Holland. While on board, he begged the captains to let him work with the sailors so he could learn the trade. It was rare that a sailing ship had a refined young man who wanted to work like a commoner so both the Captain and the crew were amused enough to let Sam help and learn. Over time Sam learned enough to discuss sailing but not enough to be called a sailor.

Everyone at the docks knew that Sam could read and write as he was constantly running merchant letters to the various captains and carrying letters he sometimes drafted for illiterate captains back to the merchants. Eventually, this same group learned that he wanted to be a sailor in the Royal Navy and he wanted to go to sea.

In 1708, the HMS Bedford Galley arrived at Exeter with an inventory for a deceased Sailor, John Chambers, which needed to be filed with the Church of England at Gainsborough, England. Sam was retained to deal with the local Church of England in Exeter to make sure this supplemental inventory would end up being appropriately transferred to his family in Gainsborough.

Sam knew how to read and write both Latin and English, which meant he could deal with the necessary church documents as both languages were still in use by the Church of England. Inventories were usually filed with Wills at the time the Will was prepared which was right after John Chambers had joined the Royal Navy. However, this was a supplemental inventory, which listing those things John Chambers had on board ship at the time of his death.

While performing his duties, Sam took every chance to talk with the Captain about his desire to join the Royal Navy. Like most young men, Sam overstated his skills and importance, which led to his being allowed to join the Royal Navy. Sam viewed this opportunity as a mixed blessing. He would be leaving Exeter, a city he loved, in exchange for joining the Royal Navy at the very lowest level.

The Captain already knew that Sam was a Christian man of good character who could read and write, so that would add to his value on board his ship. However, after talking with Sam about his sailing experience, the Captain was not certain if he would really classify Sam as an Ordinary Seaman, the term used for experienced seamen in the British Navy. However, the HMS Bedford was a sailing galley with 40 ores, and a big strong youth like Sam could easily learn to man an ore.

The deal they cut was that Sam would willingly man an oar when required, and in his idle time, he would do clerical tasks for the Captain and learn the skill necessary for Sam to develop into an Ordinary Seaman.

While he was not very excited about his proposed position he recognized that this is the only way he would have been allowed on a fifth-rate ship. The HMS Bedford Galley was a 34-gun fifth-rate galley launched in 1697, and purchased that year for Navy service. It also had 28 smaller bore swivel guns for close fighting prior to boarding an enemy ship

The fifth class designation was for very heavily armed, shallow draft, fast ships which were designated as pirate catchers because they could go wherever a small nimble pirate ship could go. When they captured a ship, the crew would all get a small piece of the prize money in addition to their regular pay. Since the positions were so desirable Prince George usually made the assignments as political favors. Sam was lucky to get the position as a galley rower even though it was literally in the bottom of the boat.

Sam felt sorry that everything he had learned about world trade would be wasted once he started his career in the Royal Navy. It would take him a few years to recognize how his knowledge of global trade would be valuable to his ability to make money.

Sam knew that everyone in his current fleet heading to the island of Saint Croix [1716] thought he became a sailor at a young age but that was not the case. He was first able to be a courtier and go to sea at the age of 17 and then only on merchant ships where he got a little experience. He finally was allowed to join the Royal Navy when he was 19 years old and as Sam tells his story, it was not much of a learning experience.

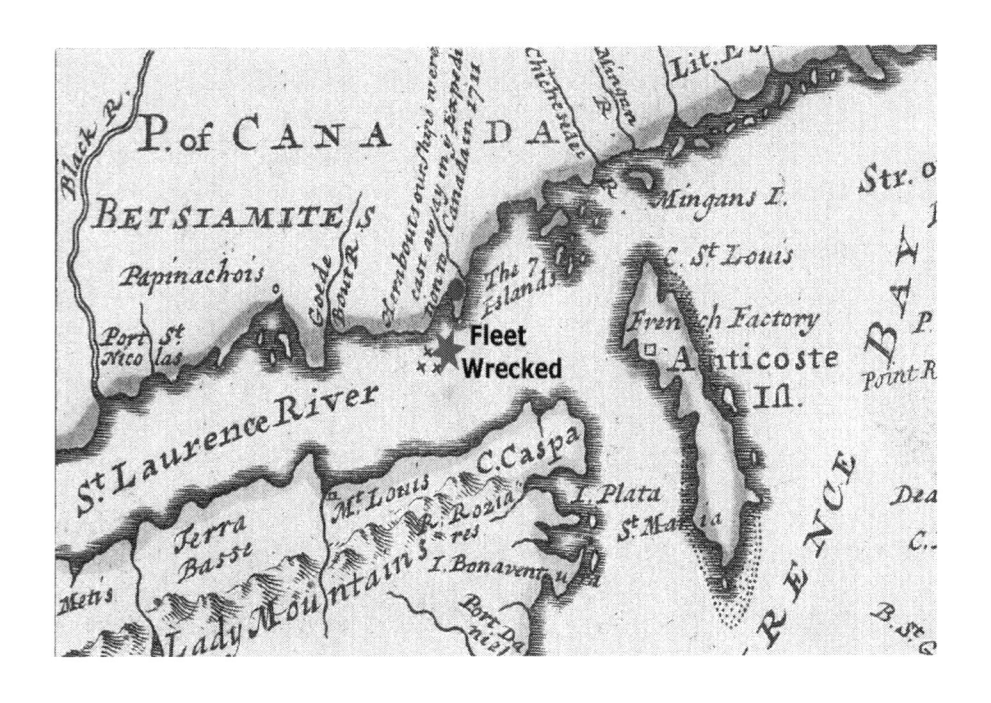

**Location of Fleet Disaster
1711 Quebec Expedition**

Chapter 3
Life in the Royal Navy

Sam was excited about going to sea as a Royal Navy Sailor. He looked forward to eliminating those disgusting pirates who knew no limits to their excessively evil criminal behavior and debauchery. As he saw his mission, he was not working for the good of the Monarchy but for the good of those global merchants who were his friends and for the good of humanity.

Captain Robert Holymann had been captain of the ship since it had launched in 1697. It had been built by Holland Shipyard in Portsmouth, New Hampshire using American oak as a fifth-rate ship and purchased by a Mr. Taylor as a gift to King William and delivered to London where Captain Holymann took command.

During the first couple of years, the captain and crew cruised the Atlantic and Caribbean feeling out the ship and chasing pirates away from merchant ships. They never captured any or even engaged any pirate ships in a serious battle. Then on February 10, 1699, Captain Robert Holymann was subjected to a Royal Navy Court Martial for the crime of allowing two pirate ships to escape and taking on goods from a merchant ship contrary to instructions.

Since he was well connected to King William and it was a time of peace, he was acquitted and returned to his ship. Sam heard the story from a few disgruntled Ordinary Seamen, but overall the crew was happy with their captain and the ship. While originally appointed as a favor from King William, Holymann eventually turned into a fairly decent Captain.

By the time Sam signed on to the HMS Bedford Galley, Parliament passed an updated Cruisers and Convoys Act in 1708 allocating regular warships to the defense of trade. This was a rather boring assignment and also limited the amount of prize money the ships could earn by capturing French or Spanish ships regardless if they were pirate, merchant or military vessels.

Captain Holymann ran his ship by the regulations and had prayer sessions twice a day and Sunday worship whenever possible for everyone not manning the ship. He also had regular training for all gunners which he personally supervised until he recognized which gunners had the best eye for the range to a target. These men were selected as the lead gunners based on their skill. There was a lead gunner for the 12 pounders and one for the 6 pounders.

Most convoys leaving Barbados for Jamaica followed a line of site course along the island chain. While cruising the Eastern Caribbean with convoys, he would occasionally sight a ship without colors. Since Holland, Portugal and England were all allies, he assumed that anyone in the area without colors was either a pirate ship or a French ship. He would use his 12 pound guns which had more than twice the range of a six pound (or smaller) cannon. He would order his lead gunner to fire a shot across the bow and send orders to the ship to heave to for inspection.

Captain Holymann had also learned to use his oars to his advantage. With three men at each oar, the Bedford Galley would move at 3 knots which was just about as fast as a small inter island trader and more maneuverable than any sailboat in poor wind.

Usually, the boats they stopped were inter-island

traders of no concern but on two occasions they found pirate sloops; one with eight cannons and the other with twelve which readily surrendered. These were disposed of with the Governor of the next English Island they passed after an inventory was taken and signed by both the Captain and the Governor with a copy for the Admiralty Prize Court. Even these two small prizes yielded a year's worth of pay for Sam after the cargo, ships and guns were sold. Of course Sam waited until he returned to England to collect the money and lived off part of his regular pay.

By the time they reached Jamaica, HMS Bedford Galley was starting to take on water. The Captain ordered the Bedford Galley to proceed to Portsmouth, Rhode Island where he thought the ship had been originally built using American oak.

There was some debate about whether a ship built of American oak was inferior to those built with English oak. Captain Holymann thought that they lasted as long as similar ships built of English oak during the post war period of hasty construction. England was trying to recover from the heavy losses at the hands of the French during the previous war and was stressing the European shipyards while rebuilding their fleet.

While awaiting orders from the Admiralty, the whole crew was put on shore leave with orders to check in once a week since repairs had not even started. While the other sailors partied at the nearby pubs, Sam explored the towns in the area. Plymouth shared an island in Narragansett Bay with Newport, which was a thriving port city that many compared to New York, Philadelphia and Boston. He explored the docks and found a few of the same captains and merchants he had met and worked with in Exeter.

What he was surprised to find was that Newport operated as a free port where ships of all nations were welcome to trade as long as everybody behaved. Pirates showed up on a regular basis and traded with merchants from all over the world and were treated as equals.

On some occasions merchants and captains actually bought back their own goods from the pirates who had robbed them. This disturbed Sam because he and his shipmates were putting their lives on the line trying to stop piracy while the merchants were treating losses as a cost of doing business and passing the cost to customers with increased prices.

During this period of moral doubt, one of his new friends invited him to Church and he decided to go. The dominant religion was Baptist, which was sort of like the nonconformists of Exeter but they stressed separation of Church and State and allowed for complete freedom of conscious in all religious matters. Thus, both Jews and Quakers had settled in the community around 1650 and were very active in business in 1709. Sam liked the Quakers but did not trust their concept of non-violence because he had met totally amoral pirates and the human scum of many ports.

He generally liked most Jewish Merchants but they never tried to preach or convert non-Jews. Thus, Sam fell into the habit of attending the Baptist Church, which was the dominant Christian religion of Newport. Sam began to see and accept their belief that it was better to deal with an evil person than to stand on principles and starve your wife and children. It was simply a pragmatic belief set where you personally worshiped the one true God, obeyed the Ten Commandments and did good deeds so long as it didn't hurt yourself.

It was during this time that Sam Bellamy became close friends with Paulsgrave Williams who he met at church and instantly liked. While Paulsgrave was a little older and established in business, when it came to world trade in the merchant community, Sam had much he could teach his friend Paulsgrave.

He introduced Paulsgrave to merchants and ships captains as an honorable silversmith. Williams did excellent work at reasonable prices for the new customers that Sam had referred. They were happy and used their reputations to refer Williams to other captains and merchants so his business grew dramatically.

After about five weeks, the Captain received an order from the Admiralty advising him that the preferred course would be to return the ship to Chatham Dockyard in Kent.

The Chatham Dockyard had already rebuilt the HMS Faulkland which was also made by Holland in America so they had experience with American materials and construction techniques. Captain Holymann questioned his orders as he did not think the HMS Bedford Galley was fit for a long voyage across the North Atlantic.

There was a delay of another month and then orders to proceed to Portsmouth, New Hampshire, for rebuilding by Holland and complete the task by 1710. The orders also included a new set of specifications for a fifth rate ship that displeased the Captain.

He was advised to proceed to Boston and drop off the most senior Ordinary Seamen at the Royal Navy Dock and to proceed to Portsmouth, New Hampshire, with a skeleton crew. After the required repairs, he was to return to Boston using the skeleton crew and await orders.

Before he left Rhode Island, he sent notice of a request to be replaced of his very desirable duty on the fifth-rate ship as he disagreed with the new specifications. Captain Holymann's complaint was that the new specifications eliminated the 12-pound cannons which he had come to rely on for their greater range. The new ordnance and configuration for armament would be a total of 32 guns, with 4 nine pounders on the lower deck, 22 six pounders on the upper deck and 6 four pounders on the quarter deck.

While it was about the same number of cannons as he was used to, it was a lot less firepower. The new Galley was being designed for close in fighting and not for support of a fleet at a major naval battle. Also, while in Portsmouth, Rhode Island, he had seen that some of the better armed pirate ships carried more firepower.

By that time, Captain Holymann had his adventure at sea and even made a little money in the process, so as a gentleman, it was time for him to retire. Of course, while awaiting the ship rebuilding, he had included Sam as a part of his skeleton crew so he could have Sam monitor the rebuilding and document it for the Admiralty. Of course Sam asked about the details of everything the shipwrights did.

When the ship was done, Captain Holymann reviewed Sam's work and signed off on the log. Sam was happy to be of service to the Captain who gave him the chance to become an Ordinary Seaman in the Royal Navy.

When the Ship was completed, Sam was impatient

until the weather stabilized enough to launch it and leave. There was absolutely nothing to do at the shipyard. The shipbuilder, Holland, was actually on New Castle Island, which Sam guessed was only a few hundred acres and about the same number of people.

The island was just off the coast of Portsmouth, which it had officially been part of until about ten years before their arrival. While the town was close by rowboat, people had to carefully choose when they went across the narrow channel to the town of Portsmouth. The Harbor has the fastest tidal current in North America and could carry you out to sea if you had problems. A rising tide and high tide was best as it slowed the current flowing down river and the two forces almost neutralized each other.

As small as New Castle Island was, Portsmouth, New Hampshire, was not much better. Sam recognized it as a fine harbor with sturdy docks, but all of the commerce was focused on lumber and fishing. A smaller industry of trading in slaves had been going on for over fifty years. Sam knew none of the captains and there were very few foreign merchants who resided in the town as lumber and fishing were seasonal enterprises.

Sam was happy to leave when the ship was launched as the next port of call was Boston. Sam got his first real sailing experience on the trip south to Boston as the wind was strong and they were now very short staffed due to a few deserters who chose to stay and marry local women. While it took less than a day to reach Boston and anchor off the Port, Sam now felt he could truly claim to be an Ordinary Seaman.

In Boston, Captain Holymann was replaced by Captain Andrew Lee and the Ordinary Seamen that didn't like and disrespected Captain Holymann loved the change. Captain Lee was a mean spirited and temperamental person who ruled his ship by fear. He yelled and swore at the sailors and would punish the men for any minor infraction. The crew was mostly new except for the skeleton crew, which had stayed at New Castle Island during the rebuilding of the ship. None of the new sailors thought that the Captain's deportment was strange or rare, they accepted it as the standard. As long as they got their rum ration every day, they could live with the Captain and his manners.

The big problem with the rum ration was not to become drunk on board as this resulted in a public flogging with a cat of nine tails in front of the entire crew. Even worse, you might be deprived of your daily rum ration for a period of time. All of the sailors were on their best behavior after receiving the rum and avoided all arguments, fights or other obvious signs of intoxication.

Under Captain Holymann, Sam avoided the half pint of hundred proof rum offered twice a day and instead was rewarded with three pence a day which he saved. [Note that is over 6 shots of 100-proof rum twice a day.] The other sailors finally convinced Sam that the rum made time pass quicker and you stopped taking the Captain's yelling and swearing seriously and just listened for a direct order which had to be obeyed.

Sam never did learn to enjoy the feeling of being drunk, so he usually gave his lunch-time portion to someone at night who had been deprived of their daily rum portion so they could sleep at night. After a few nights of sickness from drinking so much, Sam finally learned to drink his evening flask so he would sleep well every night.

As soon as the ship was ready, they sailed to the Potomac base in Virginia for routine duty. Governor Alexander Spotswood, of Virginia, took an active interest in the fleet and used them to arrange for the transport of convict labor on any ship's return from England. Virginia was a tobacco growing state with seasonal labor needs. The fact of the matter was that convict labor was cheaper than indentured labor or African slaves and the terms of duty were for seven to fourteen years. As chance would have it, the Governor sent an order on July 31, 1711 to transport 75 prisoners to Captain Lee of the Bedford Galley but it reached the Potomac base too late.

In mid June 2011, the HMS Bedford Galley was advised to come fully supplied to Boston and join a fleet being assembled for an invasion of Quebec in New France by Rear Admiral of the White, Sir Hovenden Walker. This was an ideal assignment for the Bedford Galley. Even though the galley was small, it could still carry seventy-five fighting men. It would also be able to navigate the St. Lawrence River easier than the larger ships of the line and be able to take soundings and lead the way. The whole crew was excited with proving themselves.

Admiral Walker had been promoted because of his close connections to the Queen and that was the principle reason he was chosen for this assignment over other more qualified people.

In the name of secrecy, the fleet left England with only enough provisions for a short European tour of duty. This was to deprive spies of any knowledge and even the Captains of the fleet had no knowledge of where they were going or what they would be doing. The intention was to resupply in Boston. However, nobody realized that the number of sailors, marines and personnel of the fleet exceeded the population of Boston so the fleet sat in Boston Harbor for six weeks waiting for supplies.

While the secret was out and the people of Quebec were prepared, that's not what caused the failure. It was plain old-fashioned incompetence. Sam never got the complete story until years later when his partner Olivier Levasseur explained it all. Olivier first heard it from a French Captain who had been on board Admiral Walker's boat. A disaster occurred because the English Fleet had no pilot and everybody feared Admiral Walker and would not deliver bad news.

The fleet entered the St. Lawrence using the inexperienced Captain of a French Transport ship who had agreed to act as a pilot and guide the way in exchange for freedom. They entered the river and they faced fog and shifting winds. When they started nearing the North shore during the night, the Captain told the Admiral that they were heading to a disaster. The Admiral gave the orders to turn north assuming they were approaching the south shore. The Captain blindly followed the orders including one not to wake the Admiral again.

Captain Goddard, an Army Officer, took it upon himself to wake Admiral Walker and tell him they were so close to shore he could see the breakers even in the dark and fog. The Admiral dismissed him but Captain Goddard returned and screamed that the Admiral should come see for himself or all hands would be lost. Admiral Walker saw the precarious shape the fleet was in and, after consulting with the French Captain, he ordered the lines cut and the ships to turn South. In the end the English lost eight ships with 705 soldiers, 150 sailors and 35 women.

That night [August 22, 1711], Captain Lee figured out the problem and had his men man the oars of the HMS Bedford Galley. Technically, he never abandoned the fleet but he also never allowed his ship or men to be put in harms way. While no one else in the fleet was aware of his leadership, the more seasoned Ordinary Seamen of the HMS Bedford now looked upon him as a genuine hero and ignored his bazaar behavior.

Before the fleet made the decision to retreat to England, 3 fifth rate ships, HMS Experiment, HMS Diamond and the HMS Bedford Galley were assigned to accompany a convoy of Merchant ships to Lisbon, Portugal. The trip was uneventful and the sailors were given a shore leave in Lisbon. While the other sailors partied and womanized, Sam took time to get acquainted with some of the Merchants he only knew through his correspondence from Exeter.

On their return to England, they were ordered to the port of Sheerness to wait for a pilot to take them upriver. All Sam remembered is that Sheerness was a nasty little town with blue houses filled with poor people and an understaffed shipyard. As far as Sam was concerned, this was even worse than Portsmouth, New Hampshire, which bored him to tears.

Fortunately, the stay at Sheerness was brief as the ship picked up a pilot and moved up the Medway River to Chatham, which was somewhat of an improvement. Sam stayed there for a couple of weeks while the ship was refitted, and damaged and broken items were replaced.

At Sheerness, the ship had also picked up a man who was to be the ship's Chaplin for a few months. The Captain and the Chaplin could not get along but in

Chatham, they took shore leave one Sunday and walked the village as the Captain was in a very good mood. The Reverend Giles Ransford took advantage of the situation and got permission to teach Bible studies to the young men on board.

The other issue was a little more delicate but Rev. Ransford was also successful in that. It seems that some of the warrant officers were living with women on board and they were not married to them. Rev. Giles Ransford got bold and asked the captain to have them removed, which he did.

Of course there were ramifications. At sea on the way to Spithead, the Captain and crew tormented Rev. Ransford. That is everybody except Sam who befriended him and the ships boys who he was teaching Bible studies. Truthfully, Sam thought many of the actions that tormented the Chaplin were the usual swearing and blasphemous oaths that sailors made when working but some of it might actually have been a little more aggressive especially from the warrant officers and the crews that worked with them.

However, at Spithead, Sam found out just how mean spirited the Captain could be and he felt more sympathetic towards the Reverend.

Spithead Road is an anchorage in a naturally formed inland lake of seawater connected to the sea through a narrow channel. This Road or Roadstead was being used to assemble a fleet heading to America. [Among sailors in the Caribbean, these very protected harbors are called "hurricane holes" and provide safe anchorage for sailors during storms.]

Several events occurred which disturbed Rev. Ransford and Sam was the only person on board he could talk with. It seems the Captain had the knack of reading orders and requests from the Church of England with great precision. Rev. Ransford found out about this the first time when he came on board with a request for safe passage to America. The request did not mention that he should depart in America so Captain Lee impressed him into the Royal Navy to be the ship's Chaplin. The Captain knew he was in violation of Admiralty regulations by not leading the crew in twice a day prayer or leading service on Sunday and this provided a solution.

Rev. Ransford was distressed by this change in plans but did his best on board while waiting for new orders, which would clarify where he was to leave the ship. The orders had not yet reached the constantly moving ship.

The Reverend Mr. Giles Ransford was a Gentleman from Dublin and Son of Sir Ransford formerly an Alderman of that City. He knew that he had been born to privilege but thought it was God's plan that he use his piety and education to help educate and elevate the less fortunate by using the Gospel of the Church of England as the guide.

When applying for the missionary position to go to North Carolina he acknowledged to Sam that he had overstated his credentials by asserting that he had baptized a small number of both Negroes and Indians. He also asserted that he had become proficient in the Indian's language and offered, without initial acceptance, to undertake a mission to the Americas. It seems John Urmston, the missionary in North Carolina, at this time, and no friend of Ransford, expressed deep skepticism about the latter's claims of baptizing Indians and Negroes.

This skepticism came from a very credible source.

Prior to his service as a missionary in North Carolina, Rev. John Urmston operated a school in Kensington, London, and was author of an 82 page primer that went through a number of editions.

Fortunately, Mr. Ransford *"read prayers very distinctly and with great devotion, and preached a very good useful practical sermon"* so he was hired in England to be sent to North Carolina to become Rev. Urmston's assistant. Through letters the two missionaries developed a relationship and Rev. Ransford was looking forward to working with his former adversary if he was allowed to leave the ship.

In Spithead, Captain Lee delighted in telling Rev. Ransford that Rev. Urmston was dead so he had no assignment in America and he would keep him with the ship.

One final event happened which Rev. Ransford also took as an affront. Rev. Mr. Bell, a Clergyman appointed to Virginia, had an order to come on board but his wife and servant were not mentioned in the order so the Captain barred them from boarding. The whole group was forced to stay behind and Rev. Ransford was deprived of a traveling companion and the moderating effect of having a woman on board.

Reverend Giles Ransford told Sam he believed his current trials and tribulations were God's just punishment for overstating his qualifications and he would just stay on board, trying to do God's work until released from the service.

On the way back to America, they intercepted a fairly rich French merchant ship, which they carried back to their Potomac base. It was not much of a battle. They fired one shot and the unarmed, sluggish, heavily loaded ship surrendered. The French merchant ship was loaded with sugar, indigo and cocoa. This capture was to give Sam a prize share worth three years pay or more in addition to what he had already saved with Captain Holymann.

Life got very interesting for Reverend Giles Ransford when he reached the Potomac Base. He found out that as a Chaplin, he was entitled to pay from the Church of England during his voyage as he had been working. Also, since he was working on the ship, which captured the prize, he was entitled to an Ordinary Seaman's share of the prize money.

Unbelievably, he received orders to disembark and to report to North Carolina for missionary duty. Also, Mr. Urmston was alive and had arranged transportation for him and welcomed him to stay in his home. Reverend Giles Ransford had his proof that God had forgiven him and he was on the right path to serve his God.

In May, orders came to stand down and not engage French merchants or military ships, so there would be no more rich prizes. They could still engage pirate ships but at that time it was not yet a serious problem because most had been privateers in the war and retired to live with their wealth. By the end of 1712, there was a general suspension of all military actions between France and England.

Duty reverted to the routine and they made a few trips to pick up and return with convict labor for the Virginia Colony. In the spring of 1713, they got news that that a Treaty had been signed and the war was officially over.

The HMS Bedford Galley was recalled to England for refitting, a new crew and reassignment. While it was being refitted, notice was published that many ships would be retired or placed in dry dock so any Ordinary Seaman that wanted to leave the Navy on good terms could.

Then it became official, the HMS Bedford Galley would proceed to the Indian Ocean to fight piracy as it had grown substantially in that area while Europe was at war and merchant ships were an easy target.

Sam had no interest in the Indian Ocean. He knew trade with India was almost impossible for anyone except the Sephardic Jews because there were so many cultures, middle men, governments and religions that had to be dealt with all on a system of trust built up over centuries. Indian diamonds were cut in Holland, Indian cloth was distributed through Exeter, spices were traded in London and Mediterranean red coral was controlled by Italian merchants in Leghorn. There was no room for Sam Bellamy in Indian Ocean Trade.

With the mutual consent of Captain Andrew Lee, Sam Bellamy left the Royal Navy. He was happy to leave the Captain's ship and the Captain was happy to see him go.

After collecting all his pay and prize money Sam decided to visit Exeter for awhile. He found that international trade was slow and had not recovered from the war and Indian Ocean piracy. His friend Christopher Mitchell had not been heard from since 1707 and was presumed dead along with his father.

Since there was nothing to hold him in Exeter, he decided after a short stay that it was time to go to America and make his fortune. He would use the skills he had learned, get involved with trade and become a merchant. He would start on a small scale and reinvest everything he made until he was substantial enough to buy a small house and take a wife.

The Sailor's Return

Memoirs of Captain Samuel Bellamy: 56

Chapter 4
Sam Bellamy Falls in Love

Sam had more than five years pay in savings and he decided to use his merchant friends in Exeter to safely transport his money to Boston. The merchants were glad to do it because they got the profit from a trip instantly when Sam gave them the money. The merchant in Boston would withhold an equivalent amount and keep it safely on land instead of sending cash on a risky voyage at sea. These transactions were always bonded by the merchant accepting the cash for a small fee.

In 1714, Sam decided that since he was to be dealing with merchants, he'd better learn about long voyages on a merchant ship. From his military experience, Sam knew that the voyages from England to the colonies were about twice as long as the trip back to England and it normally took about two months to get to America.

The Royal Navy kept the Ordinary Seaman in as good a shape as possible because they had to participate in battle when necessary. There were limits to their success as they did not know how to prevent scurvy, and after rations got wet, they would grow maggots and weevils. At least with hardtack (twice-baked, hard bread), you could soak your portion in tea, and skim the dead weevils off the tea before eating the softened mess. Maggots were harder to see and much more disgusting to deal with.

He had heard that sailors on merchant ships had a worse life, but he had only taken short trips across the Channel before joining the Royal Navy so had no real experience on a merchant ship. By the time his two months as a crew member on the merchant ship to America was up, he wished he had paid his own way.

It was not only the food that was bad but also the hard work you had to do on very poor rations. The boat from England was sailing into the wind so there was a need for constantly tacking and changing directions, which required a full complement of men, day and night. The Captain was not unhappy to lose some crew members in the colonies as the return trip was easier and required less manpower.

By the time he reached Boston, Sam had a modest case of scurvy, he was sunburned, wind-burned and had salt rashes all over his body from the lack of fresh water for bathing. He also had blisters from the hard work. He had lost weight and looked terrible. He was also left with a deeper understanding of the value of sailors in the Royal Navy and the lack of value in the merchant fleet.

In the seventeenth century Royal Navy, the Ordinary Seaman was an asset who could be called upon to maneuver the ship in combat and, in the worst case, fight hand to hand with the enemy. Because the Sailor was an asset, he had to be maintained in as good a shape as possible.

During this same period, the sailors manning a merchant ship were a cost of doing business, and the way to cut costs was to keep pay low and the food supply as inexpensive as possible. The only reason men ever went to sea on a merchant ship was life on land could be tougher in post-war England.

In the Royal Navy, all hands got a share of the profits from fighting pirates and capturing their ships. In the Merchant fleet, there was no benefit to the overworked, underpaid and underfed sailor actively fighting pirates. There was, however, a big potential reward for changing sides and joining the pirates when the opportunity arose.

Sam was once again faced with a puzzle. If the men were fed better would they be more loyal to the ship. Also from his previous experiences on the Boston docks, he knew that New England was a major exporter of hardtack, corn, flour, bacon, salted fish, salted pork and salted beef. Much of the food supplies went to the Southern States and the West Indies and was fed to slaves to keep them physically fit to do the hard work needed on the plantations.

To Sam, the implication was clear; the seamen in the merchant fleet had less value to the ships owner than a slave on a plantation. Sam thought there might be a business opportunity to improve the food on ships returning to Europe and turn a small profit, which he could reinvest in other business opportunities.

During his stay in Boston prior to the Quebec invasion, Sam saw the incredible ability of New England to provide food for the entire fleet in only six weeks even though there were more people in the fleet than there were citizens in Boston.

Sam knew there had to be farmers in the countryside who would sell to him at prices low enough for good quality supplies that he could resell to the ships returning to England. He would make a small profit, the Captains would provide better food for the sailors, and the sailors would have less reason to be disgruntled. However, Sam also knew that to approach people he did not know, he would have to improve his physical appearance and dress appropriately.

The obvious place for regaining his health and

improving his physical appearance was with his friend Paulsgrave Williams in Newport, Rhode Island. He purchased a wagon and horse, and took the best clothes and uniforms he had left after his release from the Navy and headed south to Newport.

He was in no hurry as he knew he had much to learn about farming and food processing in New England particularly as it related to food preservation. Along the way, he was welcomed by farmers and, in exchange for physical labor, he could usually earn a meal and a place to stay. New Englanders were currently favorable to the English who had assisted them in the French and Indian wars in the colonies while Europe was engaged in the War of Spanish Succession. Locally, the war was referred to as Queen Anne's War. They particularly liked the fact that Sam inquired about Church Services along the way and attended them frequently while traveling.

Sam's move down the coast was extremely slow. Travel on foot or on horseback between Boston and Rhode Island was very primitive due to the poor state of roads, the frequent necessity of fording streams, and the poorly constructed bridges. Usually, this method of travel was only used in cases of extreme urgency. However, the trip was not costing Sam money as he worked his way south and he had learned much from his efforts.

Farmers had stopped growing wheat along the coastal region because of mildew caused by the high humidity in the area. Wheat and corn had been the principal products for many years, and after the mildew problems, farmers substituted corn, rye, oats, potatoes, and roots. However, most of the men were pursuing greater wages earned from jobs at sea, especially fishing. Crops along the coast were grown to serve the needs of the families who grew them and the villagers who lived close to the farms. Therefore, not much would be available for Sam to purchase.

Because of the attraction, and also, the dangers of life at sea, there was a shortage of men, as many left the farms and some never returned. This was just as it had been on his way to Exeter. Sam had no trouble finding food and lodging in exchange for his labors along the way. When he reached Cape Cod, he found that the community was almost entirely Quakers who were not as well received as they were in Newport. The only Christian Church he heard of was a dissenter church committed to reforming the Church of England led by Reverend Roland Cotton of Sandwich.

He arrived on Saturday only to find that Rev. Cotton had left early to preach in the town of Barnstable, which was without a church. Many of the older people were concerned that the Quakers were seeking conversions among the true Christians and that the young people were in danger of loosing their faith in Jesus. Sam decided to go to Barnstable and hear the service of Rev. Cotton.

After the service was over, John Hallett introduced himself, Sheriff Shubael Gorham and Judge John Otis. They came to inquire about his business in Barnstable and if his intentions were honest, to welcome him to town.

Sam briefly explained his life experiences and future desires. John Hallett invited the entire party to his house for a light supper and offered Sam a room for a week of rest in exchange for his knowledge of world trade and the inner workings of the Royal Navy. Sam delighted the group with his stories of the piety and competence of Captain Holymann who had been appointed by the prior King, and contrasted Holymann to the total incompetence of Admiral Walker who led the Quebec invasion. He also told the group how the people of Boston were forced to find supplies for the fleet and suffer the arrogance of Admiral Walker and his officers for six weeks until the task was done.

He also described the brutal, blasphemous rule of Captain Lee which many seasoned sailors preferred to the piety of Captain Holymann. In either case, life on board a Royal Navy Ship was superior to life on a westward bound merchant ship and Sam declared he would never do that again as a sailor.

Every night that Sam was there, the same group met and was joined by John's son, Samuel Hallett who was just a year younger than Sam. There was also John's wife, Mercy, and young daughter, Maria, but they never joined the group or paid any attention to Sam except during meals where polite conversation was exchanged with Mercy. Maria was quiet and rarely noticed among the adults.

Sam was questioned as to his family in England. The Halletts were descended from a line of Gentlemen from Dorset, England, and John wanted to know if Sam was descended from the noble family of Belleme who arrived in England during the Norman Conquest. In the 1700's there were still many fine Gentlemen named Bellamy from the county of Devonshire, which was adjacent to Dorset, England. Sam acknowledged knowing of the families but was not aware of a close relationship.

John Hallett was very proud of his family and he knew from the Calvinist beliefs of the Puritan religion that he was predestined to serve God and his family well. He was already the second richest man in

Yarmouth only exceeded in land holdings by his oldest brother who was 33 years older. Andrew, Jr., his brother, had a big head start in building the family fortune.

John had been elected as a town selectmen to govern his community and had been appointed to the committee to build a new school and find a teacher. He was glad to find that Sam was well educated and well read.

John loved to tell the story that his father, Andrew II, was so well off in both England and America that he had to pay taxes on his land holdings to both the King of England and Plymouth Colony, which governed Yarmouth. He also told the story about his father being so frugal that he signed up with a cooper, Richard Wade, to come to America as his indentured servant. It seems that if he came as a gentleman, he would have had to pay his own fare, as well as that of his wife and children.

Andrew II bribed the cooper to list him as his indentured servant in exchange for paying one-half of his fare to America. Thus, Andrew Hallett was able to transport his entire family to the colonies for only one-half of one fare instead of the four fares he should have paid. Since he was a person of substance, he never had to serve a day as an indentured servant in Plymouth Colony.

In Plymouth Colony, wealth was treated as a sign of God's Blessing and had to be respected. John Hallett was treated as an English Gentleman and called Mr. Hallett by everyone except his closest friend and family. Sam left Yarmouth thinking he had met another person who would mentor him especially when John asked Sam to come and visit him on his return trip to Boston and bring all the commercial news from Newport.

As Sam went further south along the New England coastal communities, he found more of the same social conditions. The men had gone to sea and the women were left behind to grow family and community gardens. Sam came to realize he would have to take an inland route north to Boston on his return to Boston if he was to find any farmers with ship's stores to sell to his new business.

Sam reached Newport in the fall of 1714 in pretty good condition but had many questions. So far he had found no support for his business model of providing the produce of New England farmers to ships returning to England. Simply stated, there was no excess of produce along the coastal route he had chosen in moving south to Newport.

When Sam reached Newport, Paulsgrave Williams convinced him that he should spend the winter in Newport, rebuild his strength and then head north along a more westerly route and interact with farmers who were less likely to compete with the fishing industry.

Of course, Sam sought out his natural comfort area along the docks and started doing odd jobs for captains and merchants. He wrote letters, acted as a courier, and even started investing in a small part of a ship's cargo. He earned enough money to feed his horse and even managed to save a little bit more.

In the spring of 1715, Sam started north to Boston taking a westerly course but the roads were no better. He met a few farmers who were planning to grow excess crops but none who were wiling to commit to a contract in advance of the harvest. Thus, after Sam returned to Boston, he had no way to commit to ships' captains, and decided to seek advice from his friend John Hallett.

As the door to the Hallett Family home opened, two people stood staring at each other in totally shocked silence. Sam saw a stunningly beautiful young woman who he found out was a more mature Maria who had blossomed during the eight months Sam was down in Newport with Paulsgrave Williams. Maria saw a very stylishly dressed, handsome, Sam Bellamy who was now completely healthy and had an air of affluence and success.

Sam went to town and met with John and Samuel Hallett and told them he had been to the house and met Maria who was quite the beauty. Since she was home alone, Sam did not feel it proper that he stay. John Hallett continued to be impressed by the piety and excellent manners of the impoverished Ordinary Seaman he had taken pity on eight months earlier.

Unknown to Sam until later in the week, Maria was having a constant battle with her father. She thought she was old enough to plan her future. Her Aunt Anne, wife of Andrew Jr., got married when she was 13 and had twins when she was 14. She was so young and healthy she went out and gathered eggs the very same day while her mother, who was only 29, watched her babies. Andrew Jr. was fifteen years older than she was.

Her uncle Joseph married his wife when she was 18 and he was 36. Thus, he was eighteen years older than his wife. Her grandfather, Andrew Sr., married his wife Mary when she was 15. Maria had been named for her paternal grandmother. Her father, John Hallett, got married when there was a shortage of

Memoirs of Captain Samuel Bellamy: 65

suitable young women in Barnstable and Yarmouth and married her mother, Mercy, who was age 23 in 1681, and considered a spinster.

Maria had wanted to get married to an older man for some time because that was very consistent with her family history and it seemed to work well for everyone. The problem was there was now a vast shortage of qualified men in the area. The sons of poorer land-holders had gone to sea. Many of the others had forsaken Jesus and joined the Quakers, who the Puritan's were fighting and sometimes hanging for heresy. Her father wanted nothing to do with poor people as that was an obvious sign that they were not God's chosen people and that was almost as bad as being a Quaker.

Maria decided to pursue Sam in her own manner as her father seemed to like Sam and she usually got her way.

Meanwhile in town, a discussion of religious tolerance had come up and the Quakers and Jews were the issue. Sam pointed out that in Exeter, England, Lisbon, Spain, Leghorn, Italy, and Newport, Rhode Island, people of all religions and countries cooperated to the mutual benefit of everyone engaged in trade. Sam knew from this cooperation and competition that there was a greater variety of trade goods and generally lower prices for these communities. For ports like Boston that focused on lumber and fishing, many items were unavailable and, when delivered by coastal shipping, prices were higher.

John Hallett stood his ground particularly with his contempt of the Quakers. Nobody in the Plymouth Colony liked serving as an alderman, sheriff or judge because they had their own business to attend to and these were unpaid positions of civic duty. The Quakers were exempt because they would not swear an oath. The Quakers refused to fight in any wars, so while John Hallett was a Corporal under Capt. John Gorham in 'King Philip's War,' the Quakers were busy making money while he was protecting them from the Indians. They also were exempt from paying taxes to support a town minister like Rev. Cotton, which raised the cost for every law abiding Christian who was paying his taxes.

The Quakers were a growing group who were actively proselytizing and recruiting new members among the children of the original settlers. The benefits to converts were obvious; no public service, no fighting in war, lower taxes and worship your own personal God as you thought best, which set a very low standard for some people.

Sam could understand John Hallett's point of view but it posed another one of those moral questions Sam would have to ponder at some time in the future. The group returned to John's house for a light supper and more conversation and exchange of ideas.

Over the next couple of days, John and Mercy noticed their daughter seeking out and spending more time with Sam in deep conversation. They didn't really think much about it because of the piety and good manners of Sam Bellamy who they still looked upon as an impoverished Ordinary Seaman.

Maria was totally enthralled with Sam's stories and life experiences as she had spent her whole life on Cape Cod and never even made it to Boston. Sam behaved as a perfect gentleman as he knew that he would have plenty of time to court a woman after he made his fortune.

On the third night, Maria took total control and sneaked into Sam's bed and freely gave herself to him. At first Sam thought it was a wonderful dream and put it out of his mind. When she came to him on the fourth night, he knew it was real. On the morning of the fifth day, they talked about it and agreed that Sam should ask for her hand in marriage and they both went to see John.

When Sam started to speak and request Maria's hand in marriage, John lost his temper and shouted at Sam. He accused him of a serious breach of trust as he had taken into his house a half-dead impoverished seaman from a merchant ship. Now that he had recovered and had a little success, he returned to John's house as a fortune hunter trying to wed and bed his daughter. John ordered him to leave his house immediately while he went for his friends Sheriff Gorham and Judge Otis. If Sam was there when he returned or ever came back to Cape Cod again, he would have him hung for violating church law. Samuel Hallett warned Sam that the threat was real and he should leave his father's house immediately.

Sam left right away and started heading back to Newport. Along the way, the charge of being a "fortune hunter" really bothered him as he wanted nothing more in life than to be an honest merchant and make Maria Hallett his wife. After a while a plan began to form in his mind and when he recognized his new plan, he burst out laughing for the first time since he left Cape Cod.

**Sir William Phips
First Royal Governor
of the
Province of Massachusetts Bay**

Chapter 5
Sam Plans to be a Treasure Hunter

While upset and dwelling on the insult that John Hallett had called him a fortune hunter, Sam started thinking of the most famous and successful treasure hunter of recent memory, Sir William Phips. He was born a commoner and was one of over a dozen living children his mother had with her two husbands.

Before he died, he was a successful businessman, a treasure hunter who found a fortune, Knighted by the King of England, appointed Chief Sheriff for all of New England and later Governor of the Massachusetts Bay Colony. He also led a successful invasion of Canada during King William's War. Despite his crude manners and violent temper, he was often admired for his heroic accomplishments in the face of adversity.

Every person in New England knew the story. Cotton Mather had written a booklet about his life that was widely circulated in England and New England. His story was also told by sailors at sea and, for a while, every ship during the War of Spanish Succession seemed to have a sailor who claimed to know William Phips and to have sailed with him.

Depending on who was telling the story, a different aspect of his life was always stressed.

His political opponents complained that he frequently quarreled with friends, foes, and other government officials. His behavior was described as "blustering aggressiveness" and his contemporaries complained of his "lowness of education".

Cotton Mather described his piety and his fidelity to his wife and used him as an example of God's rewards for a just man regardless of his status at birth.

The sailors all loved him because he was a lax, but just, captain who would rarely punish minor infractions. When some sailors were on the verge of mutiny, he quelled the mutiny and stopped at the next port and got rid of the malcontents. When they finally found treasure, he promised shares to every man on board even if he had to pay them from his own share.

Regardless of the opinions, there were basic facts that everybody agreed upon.

As a youth, he helped raise sheep on the family farm, and then, at eighteen years old, he became apprenticed as a ship's carpenter and started life on his own. Upon completion of his apprenticeship, he moved to Boston and worked in a shipyard until he got married. He then moved back to Maine and started a shipyard. In the same year, the King Phillip Indian War broke out. Despite the threats, he was very successful building many small ships for fishing and delivering coastal fright.

Since he was already in the lumber business for his own shipyard, he decided to build a larger merchant ship and deliver local lumber to Boston's shipyards. Just as he finished his own merchant ship and had gathered the lumber, the town came under attack from Amerindians. Instead of loading the lumber, he loaded all the town's people on board and left for Boston where he was received as a hero.

Despite the fact that the Indians destroyed everything he owned, and that he was illiterate and now bankrupt, many Boston Merchants supported his effort to build a shipyard and invested in his venture. After five years of successful shipbuilding, Phips, once again, got anxious for a greater payday and decided to engage in a wrecking venture.

In wrecking, an adventurer would try to find sunken ships by any means possible and then engage divers to recover anything valuable from the wreck. By 1682, wrecking was an established industry in several locations in the Caribbean.

The Florida Indians were probably the first to engage in this activity in the Western Hemisphere because they were already free diving on the reefs for conch and, when they happened upon a wreck, they recovered anything of value they desired.

The Spaniards quickly picked up on this activity and started professional recovery operations for their sunken ships. Lucayan Indians who dove the reefs in the Western Caribbean, and Africans, who had been engaged in diving for Venezuelan pearls, were redeployed to dive for sunken Spanish treasure.

The Spaniards had divers and ships waiting to be used in recovery efforts in many major ports around the dangerous waters of Florida, Hispaniola, Cuba, Bermuda and the Bahamas. When the English took over Bermuda, wrecking became a major industry for colonists.

Before William Phips, most wrecking operations were based on direct knowledge of a sunken ship, as the Spanish would have had, or just plain luck of spotting a ship going down at sea, like those living on Bermuda or the Bahamas would know about.

On his first trip, Phips went to the Bahamas where the English wrecking industry was then centered. While in the Bahamas, he found there was too much competition and no compelling reasons for locals to share information with a Boston Captain. Still, by searching for coins on the beaches, and diving on the reef offshore, he managed to find enough coins for his investors to earn a small profit.

On his second voyage, he got financing from London including King Charles II. He left in 1683 and spent two years diving off Jamaica and Hispaniola. He discovered enough treasure to allow him to stay at sea for two years. He then returned to London with all investors suffering a small loss but not enough to deter investors from lining up for his third and greatest expedition.

King James II, who had just taken the throne after his brother's death, refused to participate but did not stand in the way. He issued a patent for the venture to the Duke of Albemarle, who assembled a group of investors to fund Phips' third expedition. The expedition had two ships: the James and Mary, a 22-gun 200-ton frigate, and the 45-ton Henry of London, a sloop commanded by Francis Rogers who was Phips' second mate on the previous unprofitable voyage.

The ships sailed from London in September 1686, and arrived off Hispaniola two months later when the weather was bad. The search did not get started until the weather settled down enough for the divers to work in clear water. In January 1687, Phips sent the smaller ship under Captain Rodgers to search the banks and reefs northeast of Hispaniola. The ship returned in early February with evidence of a major find.

For the next two months, the divers and ships' crews worked to recover treasure: gold and silver bullion, doubloons, jewelry, and other valuables. Concerned about the possibility of a jealous crew, Phips promised the sailors, who had been hired for merchant seaman's wages, that they would receive shares in the find even if he had to pay them from his own percentage. When finished, the ships sailed directly to England without stopping along the way.

Phips reported recovering £300,000 worth of treasure from the wreck. After Albemarle, and all the other share holders were paid, Phips received £19,000. A man of his word, he paid £8,000 in crew shares leaving him £11,000. Phips and the crew were presented with medals and Phips was knighted by King James II in June. This was accompanied by political appointments in New England.

As a personal favor to the new King, Phips agreed to return to the site of the wreck on an expedition funded by the King. His heart was not in this venture as he thought he had not been well rewarded for his previous efforts and on this expedition his expected share was even less. However, he was grateful for his title and his new position so he went as requested.

In September 1687, Phips returned to the wreck even though he did not command the venture. Admiral Narborough of the Royal Navy personally elected to lead the expedition and King James provided a navy frigate for security. When they arrived, they found the wreck had been discovered by others, and the frigate scattered several smaller ships working in the area.

Arriving in November, Phips stayed for the new year despite rough seas that slowed their progress. In early May just as operations were starting to yield treasure, he got permission to leave the expedition and return to New England to his wife and the new position as Provost Marshal General for New England.

Phips left in early May. Shortly thereafter Admiral

Narborough died and the Captain abandoned the search returning with a small profit of only £10,000. Fortunately, King James II was deposed by the end of 1688 so there were no negative consequences from his abandoning the King's Wrecking Expedition.

Phips got totally immersed in New England politics. He had more money than he would need for the rest of his life, he was now Sir William and his wife Lady Mary, and the only time he went to sea again was on military campaigns against New France in King William's War.

On the rest of the trip to Newport, Sam dreamed day and night about becoming a successful wrecker, making a fortune and being knighted. Of course, the practical side of Sam knew he would have to find out all he needed to know to insure success.

His biggest advantage was that on his visit to Lisbon on the HMS Bedford Galley, he had become aware that the Dutch Sephardic Jews of the Leghorn Network had in 1703 been able to smuggle to Lisbon from Spain information on the routes used by the Spanish Fleet to move treasure from Central and South America back to Spain.

The message he had delivered to a member of the Leghorn Merchants on his return to Chatam, England, was to give a broad overview of the routes and to let his contact know that a map was being prepared to assist privateers in their war efforts. However, to be most valuable, the map would need to include wind directions and currents, in addition to the actual course, and this would take some time to compile.

This message was conveyed verbally because of the importance of this knowledge. Also, it would be less likely to fall into French or Spanish hands if carried by a lowly sailor on an English Military vessel than if a normal commercial courier was used. Sam never told anyone about this mission as it was too sensitive and nobody outside the Leghorn Network would know this valuable commercial information existed.

Now he would have to use all his contacts to get a copy of that map. If he knew the routes, wind and current, he would have a good chance of finding where the ships were being blown off course during storms and where they might have sunk.

His plan was to get a copy of the map, arrange for a ship, provision it and head for Jamaica to recruit divers and a navigator familiar with the sea in the area of greatest probability of treasure. He knew that this venture would require every cent he had and impact his future success and his ability to marry Maria Hallett which was now in God's hands.

The Serrana Banks

Chapter 6

A Rough Start to a Good Plan!

Sam's first attempt at treasure hunting was horrible. He thought he was getting the best of advice from his friend Paulsgrave but the trip turned into a disaster due to his new partners. He started out with a plan that included writing to his friends in the Leghorn Network and inquiring about the Spanish shipping map.

He got a reply in about five weeks on his request for the map of the Spanish treasure fleet routes and his correspondent reminded him of his pledge to secrecy of his source of information on the routes used by the treasure fleet. The merchant from Lisbon also explained that the detailed map was still a secret, as the copper plates to print the map were not completed until after the end of the War of Spanish Succession.

The Leghorn community all felt that the best use of the map would be to hold off printing multiple copies of the map until a future war when privateering was a more certain profit making venture than treasure hunting.

On a personal note, Sam's merchant contact thought that Sam already knew enough about the route to recognize that the Serranilla Banks off the coast of Honduras would be the best place to look and the area North of Hispaniola would be the worst. After William Phips found his fortune, there were 20 to 30 wreckers a day working the North side of Hispaniola with little success.

The course along the north coast of Hispaniola had not been used as a path for the Spanish treasure fleet for decades before the Phips' discovery because convoys going from Havana to Bermuda and then east to Spain were less likely to encounter pirates, privateers or severe storms. Phips was extremely lucky.

If there were no treasure ships in the area, there would be no sunken treasure to recover. At the time of Phips' discovery, the ship that he found had been underwater and untouched for almost fifty years.

Few had ventured to search off the coast of Honduras where the shoals are located because of the extreme hazards involved in sailing and diving among the reefs. Also, the proximity to the treasure route and Spanish fleet would leave the treasure hunters exposed to attack by the Spanish Navy. Eventually, Sam's expedition did not fail for a lack of a map, it failed because of the trust he placed in his new partners.

Paulsgrave convinced Sam it would be wiser to plan on two expeditions but to do that he would need to find a partner with a ship. Sam could buy the provisions and ships stores and the Captain would provide the ship and crew. They would then risk about the same amount of money with the Captain paying the crew and Sam feeding them for the two-month journey at sea. Sam would also pay the divers and local pilot.

Paulsgrave introduced Sam to the Wanton brothers who had been described to him as Quaker merchants and ship owners who might like to join forces with him in his venture. Sam was reluctant because the non-violent Quakers would not seem to be a match for a treasure hunting expedition where defense against pirates was recognized as necessary since the discovery by Sir William Phips.

When he met the brothers in Newport, Sam instantly liked them. The brothers had an extensive list of accomplishments for being so young. John was 33 and William was 35. Both brothers were elected to represent Newport in the House of Deputies and were very different than the Quakers of Cape Cod.

As merchants, they engaged in the triangular trade and financed ships to carry rum to Africa to trade for slaves and gold; the ships carried the slaves to the West Indies to trade for molasses that was then carried back to Newport and sold to New England distillers.

In appearance, they looked like any other Newport merchant and did not dress in the simple attire of the Quakers of Cape Cod. Also, in contrast to their Cape Cod Brethren, they were not above paying taxes, taking an oath and serving in public office. Moreover, all of their merchant fleet was armed and able to defend themselves against pirate attacks.

The brothers were also willing to personally defend their colony by any means necessary. John was in control of a fleet of two armed sloops that were used to protect the outlying islands in the vicinity of Newport including Block Island, the home of Paulsgrave's mother and siblings.

During Queen Anne's War, William achieved the rank of Major for the Islands. His younger brother John, who was generally more aggressive, rose to the rank of Colonel after he attacked a French privateer who wounded one of his men before escaping. Newport was otherwise unmolested during Queen Anne's war.

Sam was no match for the brothers' negotiating skills

and a deal was quickly made where the brothers would keep two thirds to pay for the use of the armed sloop and the crew with John as Captain and Sam would provision the sloop to sail for the targeted search area, which Sam was, of course, evasive about.

Sam would get to keep one third of all the treasure they found and get all bragging rights in the colony and England if treasure was found where Sam said it was. Paulsgrave would hold Sam's information and make it public upon their return so it would be Christian honor that decided the bragging rights. Sam and Paulsgrave attended the same church and Quakers in Rhode Island generally accepted Christ as savior and the Bible as a divine work.

The trip to Jamaica to find a pilot and divers was uneventful if a little bit boring. All the sailors on Captain Wanton's sloop were from Newport. They all knew each other and had all sailed together in the Colonial Militia under Colonel Wanton to defend the harbor. On the way to Jamaica to gather a pilot, divers and additional food, they treated Sam as a partner of Captain Wanton in the great treasure adventure.

They learned that Sam had been an Ordinary Seaman in the Royal Navy on a fifth rank pirate chaser which had captured several prizes so the sailors of the sloop held him in high esteem. Occasionally, Sam would work with the crew and they got to know each other.

While in Jamaica, Sam met John Julian who had the appearance of an African. He wanted to join Sam's treasure hunt. At first, Sam assumed he was an experienced pearl diver from the oyster beds just to the north of Venezuela who had been set free as the pearl beds were no longer productive. However, he looked way too young to be an experienced diver. In very poor English, John Julian explained that he was the son of a Miskito Mother and an African Father born in Honduras along the Caribbean Coast.

Under Spanish law, children of Indian women were born free regardless of the father's race or status. John Julian had spent his entire life in a coastal village harvesting food from the cays and islands along the coast and among the reefs and shoals offshore.

The coast was very rich with seafood because many Indian villagers had died from the Spanish diseases and the sea, which used to provide food for ten families now only had to feed one. Life was easy for free Indians along the coast and he had plenty of time to explore the sea, cays, offshore islands and shoals.

At low tides in the Serranilla Banks, you could count 17 small cays but when the tide came up, all but 3 or 4 disappeared depending on sea swells. This was the area of ship-wrecks and treasure. John Julian knew of several wrecks in the area but was only used to diving in shallow waters. To go deeper, they would need experienced pearl divers or wreckers and John Julian led Sam to these men.

While awaiting the food and ships supplies, Sam spent his days teaching John Julian better English so he could communicate with him more easily. They spent time with the divers and Sam promised everyone shares from his portion when they found and recovered the treasure.

Over the course of time, Sam learned that John Julian had Anglicized his name from Juan after the English started working with the Miskito Indians as allies in their wars against Spain. John grew up in his

Mother's village and he knew nothing of his father except that his second name, Julian, was his Father's name. As a child of an Indian woman, he was a free subject of Spain and it was expedient of the British to accept the existing rules of family and freedom.

John arranged for Sam to meet four African divers now living in Jamaica and occasionally working as wreckers for hire. Sam learned that the Africans, who had worked together as a team on other occasions, had assumed African nicknames that were meaningful to the group and still easy for the Europeans to pronounce correctly. In fact, Sam came to understand that their assumed names matched the important characteristics of each man.

Gamba was the warrior. He carried himself with a fierce deportment as if always ready to attack. His eyes were constantly searching his surroundings for humans who were either friends or potential foes. He would only let down his hostile attitude when he was surrounded by friends, who he trusted, and there were no outsiders around.

Shumba was the Lion and there was no doubt about his courage or cunning as a hunter. When Gamba signaled potential threats, Shumba started evaluating the terrain for the best plan of action with the greatest element of surprise. Even as a man of courage, Shumba followed the leadership of Simba, the other lion in the Group.

Simba means "The King of the Jungle" and he was the natural leader of the four pearl divers and wreckers.

The forth member of the group was Baba and he was indeed as courageous as the rest and as proficient a free diver. However, the characteristic he was named for was his wisdom. In any given situation, he would completely analyze the situation and point out concerns and problems. Simba would not always follow his advice, but he always listened and adapted his plan of action when possible. Baba meant Father with a sign of respect for great wisdom learned through careful analysis or life long experiences.

When the ship was ready to leave, Sam went for his crew of four African divers and John Julian the Indian who appeared African. That's when Sam's troubles began.

Of all New England Colonies, Rhode Island had the longest history of engaging in the slave trade, the greatest number of imported slaves, the highest number of enslaved Africans, the greatest ratio of enslaved Africans to white colonists and subsequently the most severe laws against slaves and Free Colored people.

The crew had never seen Black men treated as anything but inferiors and now their ability to find a fortune depended on an all Black group of specialist who acted superior.

Before a mutiny started, Captain Wanton pulled Sam aside to find out what was going on and how he found these men. Sam explained that all of the divers for Phips were either Lucayan Indians or Africans and Sam thought the Captain being from New England would have known that fact.

The Captain accepted what Sam had said, but he had never addressed the humanity of enslaved Africans Everybody in the business treated the newly enslaved Africans as animals who had to be starved and beaten into submission before they could be sold to actually do work. It was like breaking a horse before it could be ridden or trained to pull a wagon. The concept of a free horse was never a concern of anyone.

As Sam pointed out to the captain and crew, if they wanted to go wrecking, they would have to trust and work with these men as there were no white divers in the West Indies like there were in the Mediterranean. On the way to the coast of Honduras, everybody was reasonably cordial, although the only person who talked with the Africans and John Julian was Sam.

Before heading to the shoals, they stopped just north of Bluefields, a pirate enclave up to the War of Spanish Succession. By that time, Spain was so weak, that the British established a colonial government for the Miskito Coast and they recognized the Miskito Indians as allies.

The purpose of this stop was for John Julian to acquire a canoe. As was common among the Indians of this era, John Julian was able to get the canoe and three friends to come along and assist him in his great adventure at no additional cost to Sam. This is the way the indigenous people of the West Indies naturally worked together.

As they prepared to leave the Indian village north of Bluefields, John Julian stayed with the ship and the other Miskito Indians left with the canoe the night before. As Sam found out, it was their plan to paddle all night long and use a light sail and rest during the hot day.

After a night and day at sea, the Africans decided to join the canoe and help paddle even though the Indians were having no problem keeping up with the sailing ship.

It seemed that Captain Wanton wanted to trim the

sails at night and double the watch as he did not fully trust the African-Indian navigator, John Julian. This slowed the voyage enough that the Indians had no trouble keeping ahead. Now with the help of the African divers paddling the canoe, they had a hard time not getting too far ahead.

The plan developed by John Julian with the consent of Sam and the Africans was to make the Serrana Banks their first stop. From Sam's memory, this group of coral reefs and cays was not even mapped by the Spanish, because it was much further west from the main route between Cartagena where ships left carrying South American Silver to go to Havana which was the staging area for the treasure fleet to return to Spain.

The plan was to work the Serrana Banks for four days so that everyone could get used to working as a team before going to dive on the more dangerous Serranilla Banks.

At the rather slow pace that Captain Wanton sailed, it took four days to reach the Serrana Banks. The ship was directed by John Julian to approach Southwest Cay from the West as there was a deep hole that provided a good anchorage which had a grassy bottom and relatively steep sides which secured the anchor.

Southwest Cay is a small island only ¼ mile long and half as wide. While it is only ten feet tall on average, the sand dunes on the south and west side of the island were thirty feet high and enough to shelter the ship from the wind and current.

During the days that Sam's crew searched for treasure, the sailors landed on the island and harvested hundreds of birds eggs for food. There was no water on the island and only a few coconut palms but they were able to pick enough nuts for their short stay.

The Serrana Banks consist of a three sided reef. The southward facing portion is the longest and runs from Southwest Cay to a break in the reef between Narrow Cay and South Cay. About half way between Southwest Cay and Narrow Cay there is a bend in the reef as it changes direction from Northeast to a more Easterly path.

Just to the north of the cut in the reef lies Little Cay. The reef then continues East until it reaches a second cut in the reef at East Cay. After this cut, the reef makes a half circle and returns west to North Cay. The interior of the reef defined by the half circle to the east and an imaginary line to the north of Little Cay has significant patch reefs and is relatively shallow. The patch reefs would hold any wrecks that occurred in this area and the shallow depth was fine for the divers who could clearly see the patch reefs on the bottom.

Unfortunately for treasure hunting, the current became fast and furious around the reef openings as the tide changed. The wall of water behind the reef could only exit between the two cuts as the tide went out. This created rip tides that are faster than a man can swim much like the tides that Sam faced in Portsmouth, New Hampshire. There are no other major breaks in the reef other than the two just described at Narrow Cay and East Cay.

The wreckers started a systematic search of the Serrana banks. They took a path from Southwest Cay to North Cay with a lookout on the front of the Canoe, and John Julian at the rear making adjustments to keep a straight course. Sam sat at the front just behind the lookout and didn't play much of a roll in the operations except as an observer.

The divers sat side by side and worked in pairs. While one was in the water the other watched for sharks and other dangers. Each diver in the water was attached by a rope and the partner in the boat tugged on the rope for any danger. The diver in the boat also kept track of time and tugged on the rope after a minute to let his partner know it was time to return to the surface. Then it was the next divers turn to dive.

Each pair of divers also had heavy rocks that they could use to carry them to the bottom faster if the water was deeper than 30 feet. This did not happen in the area of the Serrana Banks searched by Sam's team.

In the first two days, their pattern took on the shape of a fan. They would start at Southwest Cay, and head towards North Cay. They would stay inside the reef and move about 35 feet to the East before returning to Southwest Cay and repeating the process. After a few passes, they began to focus on the patch reef area northeast of Little Cay.

On the third day, they woke up to find no wind and little current. There was almost no surf and the sea was calm both inside and outside the reef. This is a rare condition for winter in the Caribbean Sea and not predictable. Still, the Africans and Indians who were familiar with the conditions decided that they could cover more ground with a reef walker.

Gamba was most adept at walking the reef and he wrapped his feet in sea calf leather and started walking from Southwest Cay towards Narrow Cay on the flat reef tops. Eventually some of the sailors noticed Gamba "walking on water" and they swore they were watching a demon in action. Sam tried to assure them he was just a man doing his job the best way he knew how.

That night the Africans and Indians stayed on the island and the crew on board grumbled all night. The next day, Sam knew he had to do something to calm them down so he told the group he was also going to walk the reef with Gamba to prove that normal men could learn the task.

They would be walking the reef between South Cay and East Cay looking on both sides of the reef. They hoped to find lighter parts of a ship among the patch reef to the north or heavier metal parts and treasure on the outside so they had to watch in both directions as they walked along the reef. The rest of the team would parallel the two reef walkers in the canoe on the inside of the reef.

Sam spent the early part of his day of reef walking just trying to keep alive. If he fell off the reef, he would most likely suffer the pain of being scratched by coral. Also he would suffer more pain trying to get back on the reef. If he bled more than a little, he might attract sharks to the area making going backward or forward along the reef top more dangerous.

By the time they reached the second cut in the reef at East Cay, Sam was quite adept at walking the reef. He acted as a lookout and never tried diving, as he feared cutting himself getting back on the reef and drawing sharks from his blood in the water.

Just as they were reaching East Cay, the group in the canoe saw some wreckage among the patch reef inside the atoll. They were diving on it so Gamba focused on looking towards the south for treasure.

Despite the sun in his eyes, which obscured his vision of the sea, Gamba saw a glitter of metal on the bottom and dove into the water. At that point, Sam notice an unusually large rogue wave coming at them which would hit Gamba as he entered the water slamming him into the reef.

Sam held on to the reef and when the wave passed, he shouted to the canoe that Gamba was hurt and the undertow from the large wave combined with the current from the receding tide were dragging him into the deep sea.

Instinctively, Sam dove into the Sea and grabbed Gamba by the waist of his loin-cloth and dragged him towards the west away from the rip-tide. He brought him to the surface just as the canoe arrived from the cut in the reef at East Cay. Simba and Shumba grabbed Gamba and Sam helped push him into the canoe.

With little speech, they slammed Gamba into the side of the boat so his chest hit the side and his head hung lower over the water. The two lions, Shumba and Simba, hit his back with the flat of their hands until he sputtered water and quickly started breathing. John Julian and Baba pulled Sam from the water just as the sharks arrived and started circling the area.

Sam and Baba kept Gamba company on East Cay while he recovered. The rest of the team investigated the patch reefs inside the semicircle reef that enclosed the east side of the atoll. Finding nothing, they returned to Southwest Cay and had a meeting before returning to the ship.

In their meeting, the team reached a consensus that their job at the Serrana bank was complete. They knew there were no obvious wrecks in the area and not much chance of finding substantial treasure. Also, during their four days at the Serrana bank, they had developed a deep trust in each other as members of a team committed to working together to find treasure. It was now time to move on to the Serranilla Banks where the real hunt would begin.

On the way to the Serranilla Banks Sam discovered he had acquired a new bodyguard and personal man-servant regardless of the facts that that he never wanted or needed either. It seems when Gamba found out about Sam saving his life, he felt he owed his life to Sam and wanted to protect and serve him. They reached a common ground where Sam appreciated the friendship and protection but tried to avoid having a servant.

The Seranilla Banks Treasure Site

Chapter 7

Mysteries of the Serranilla Banks

The Indians, Africans and Sam had all heard of the treasure ships wrecked on the Serranilla reefs but none of the group had more than a vague idea about a chart or map of the area. Generally, it was know that the reef ran from Beacon Cay, the closest and the largest island on the Banks, towards the Northeast and the furthest cay which was simply called East Cay.

Unlike the Serrana Banks, the reef did not run in a straight line but was more serpentine in nature rising above and falling below the imaginary straight line between the two distant cays. There were several major breaks in the reef and the reef was no longer large enough or strong enough to be an effective barrier to the heavy seas and the deep ocean swells surrounding the Serranilla Banks. Therefore, on many days, it was almost as rough inside the reef in shallow water as it was outside the reef in deep water.

The Spanish had referred to the shoals as "Las Viboras" in clear reference to the snake like shape of these shoals and the deadly nature of vipers. As they approached the shoals, the captain and crew were extremely concerned as there was no first hand knowledge of the area and not even a rudimentary map as Sam had drawn for the Serrana Banks.

Their only option was to attempt to find shelter in the lee of Beacon Cay and have the wrecking crew explore the reef while the ship stood by. All of the wrecking crew thought it was worth the risk because of the known presence of treasure in the area.

In the early 18th Century, the English speaking West

Indies were alive with stories of sunken Spanish treasure around the Serranilla Banks. It was incredible that people were still recovering treasure almost 100 years after the Spanish treasure fleet sunk and most of the treasure had still never been recovered. It seemed that the area was so dangerous that most wreckers and sailors were scared to go anywhere near this haunted reef with the ghosts of so many dead sailors from hundreds of wrecks in the area.

It started in 1605 when seven galleons of the Spanish treasure fleet were struck by a hurricane in the vicinity of the Serranilla Banks. Three ships survived; two ships proceeded to Cuba and one returned to Cartagena. Four went down carrying over 8 million silver Pesos.

Since there were three surviving ships, the location at the Serranilla banks is somewhat documented. The ships that went down were the:

- **Capitana**, Sam Roque, 600 tons, Captain Ruy Lopez
- **Almiranta, Santo Domingo**, 747 tons, Captain Diego Ramirez
- **Nuestra Senora de Begonia**, 500 tons, Captain Pedro Munoz de Salto
- **San Ambrosio**, 450 tons, Captain Martin de Ormachea

Based on information from the three surviving ships, the Spanish sent out salvage teams to reclaim their treasure to no avail.

The treasure was rediscovered in 1667 by fishermen from Cuba who recovered a substantial amount of silver but were limited in what they could take by the small size of their fishing boat. They did succeed in proving the treasure was still in shallow water within reach of normal diving operations.

Bad weather and incessant heavy seas that break over the area of the reef where the treasure lies hidden beneath the sea doomed further attempts at recovery by the Spanish.

The Spanish did not give up. In 1689 they sent an 18-gun ship and a patache to work the Serranilla banks to recover the treasure but were intercepted by a French frigate. A patache is a type of sailing vessel with two masts. It has very light weight construction with a shallow draft perfect for treasure hunting among reefs, rocks and shoals of the Serranilla Banks.

The French left to resupply and when they returned to continue their search of the reef area, they found an English wrecker out of Jamaica diving on an old Galleon. The French ship was a military ship, so they started diving the same wreck without fear. The French recovered four cannons and three pedreros, which are a type of old gun.

The English sent the 14-gun 6th rater, HMS Drake, to the Serranilla Shoals to protect English interest from the French who were obviously harassing the English in their pursuit of "recovering riches from a shipwreck".

Both expeditions were interrupted by the start of another European war. British records dated August 20, 1690 documented that a wreck had been discovered and salvaged in the Serranillas and they recovered silver bars north of East Cay inside the main reef.

It appeared to Sam that both the French and British

were diving on one of the two smaller Galleons listed above and the other three ships were probably in the same area waiting to be discovered and the treasure recovered.

On the way to the Serranilla Banks, Captain Walton agreed with Sam that the ship would anchor in the lee of Beacon Cay and the wreckers would proceed to East Cay and explore the patch reefs north of the small island. The wrecking crew would spend part of the second day diving in the area and return to the ship in the late afternoon before dark.

While diving in the area, the group recovered a few silver coins but could not find any silver bars, which were probably in a pile and had turned dark with age so the piles would look much like a coral reef. They continued working as they had at the Serrana Banks with one exception. Gamba was not fit to dive so this limited the amount of work his diving partner, Baba, could safely do.

The wreckers followed their plan and returned to the boat very encouraged by their limited success with using only two divers. Before they could say anything, they were met by a very angry crew who were scared to death. This could have been called a mutiny except that Captain Walton sided with his sailors.

The essence of the argument was that the ship had spent two miserable days anchored behind Beacon Cay. The waves, sea swells and rip tides had buffeted them for two days and the eerie sounds of the winds passing Beacon Cay and through their rigging were attributed to the voices of the ghosts of sailors drowned on the shoals.

The Captain said they were leaving to go wrecking in the area north of Hispaniola with or without Sam and his current wrecking crew and no amount of treasure could make them stay. The wreckers held a conference and Sam said he had to go with the ship back to Rhode Island and that John Julian and his Indians could take the coins they had recovered and go back to their village.

They could hold the silver for when Sam returned for another try or spend it as hard earned pay. The Miskito Indians had a hard time understanding the gift of silver as all in the village took care of each other's basic needs and there was little use for European money so they decided to hold it for Sam and their next adventure.

Gamba was committed to staying with Sam and defending him from all danger just as Sam had done for him. After studying the situation, Baba decided to go with John Julian as he would be very ineffective as a diver without a partner and Gamba was not yet fit to dive. Besides he did not like or trust any of the colonists on the ship except for Sam.

Baba urged the two other Africans to give up the task as they would never be treated as equals or perhaps even rewarded for their efforts. Simba and Shumba thought they could take care of themselves and trusted Sam to deliver to them a fair share of any treasure they recovered. They decided to stay on board the ship as it headed towards the north side of Hispaniola assuming there would be a stop in Jamaica to resupply the ship.

They did not convey their plan to anyone as the two were planning to jump ship in Jamaica, which is where they started. They did not want to go to the Miskito Coast with John Julian as there was no work in that area and they did not want to go with Gamba whose sole purpose in life was to protect Sam.

Their plan fell apart when Sam told Captain Wanton that he would not buy supplies on credit in Jamaica even though he acknowledge that this might be possible. Captain Wanton wanted Sam to finance the supplies for a trip to the north coast of Hispaniola even though Sam was against the venture and could not envision any chance of success.

Sam told Captain Wanton he had no more money on board and even if he did, he would not waste it on a wrecking venture for the north side of Hispaniola. With supplies and water running short, Captain Wanton made his own decision as he took a wide birth around the West Coast of Jamaica and headed through the cut between Cuba and Haiti as if he were to use their limited rations for wrecking on the north coast of Hispaniola.

At night, after Sam went to sleep, Captain Wanton set a northerly course towards Rhode Island. Sam woke to a commotion and found that Simba and Shumba had been bound in chains and locked up in a cell below the main deck. He and Gamba were locked in their own room with an armed guard at the door.

Around noon of the following day Captain Wanton came to visit and explained the situation. As he saw it, both he and Sam had invested in a losing venture with only one chance to survive and break even. With their limited food and water they would head to New England and cut their losses.

There were three Africans on board who could be enslaved and sold to recover their losses. Two were in chains below decks and Gamba was with Sam. The two below decks would be sold to repay the Wanton investment in the Treasure hunt. Since Sam was a one third partner and attached to Gamba, he could keep him to do what he wanted.

Sam was warned that laws of Rhode Island for a freed black were not easy and Sam would be better off to keep him as a slave. At least then he could determine when and how Gamba would be punished. The courts decided on how to punish the free colored when necessary so the life of Gamba would be beyond his control if he were free.

It was all that Sam could do to calm Gamba down and get him to understand all the problems with a physical confrontation. Sam agreed that there was a possibility that they could free Simba and Shumba in a surprise attack and get enough weapons to make it an even battle. However, since almost everyone in Rhode Island knew that Sam had gone to sea with Captain Wanton, every Navy on earth would hunt them as pirates until they were destroyed.

Sam wished that Baba was still on board as he knew there had to be another safer way and Sam would love the advice of Baba. Meanwhile Sam developed a plan of his own which evolved naturally over the next few days.

Gamba had insisted he be with Sam everywhere he went and the Captain forbade it. As a compromise, Sam was allowed to take Gamba for a walk every morning so long as Gamba behaved and Sam was responsible for his actions.

On their first morning walk, Gamba was physically subservient bowing his head and avoiding all physical contact with the crew but he glared at everyone with a deep and fierce hatred in his heart, which showed through his eyes. It was as if he was memorizing the soul of every person on board to determine their personal weakness so he could kill them on some occasion in the future.

When walking in the afternoon, Sam started to hear the fears of the ignorant seamen on the ship but now instead of trying to calm them, he allowed their imaginations to run wild. The sailors were convinced that the Africans were demons that could not only walk on water, but cast a spell to make Sam walk on water.

The stories grew based on minimal facts. The sailors reported the Africans could swim underwater for hours and commanded the sharks to do their bidding. Moreover they spent so much time underwater that the dead would form an army to follow their lead whenever they chose. Neither the Africans nor the ghosts of dead sailors were afraid of the sea or sharks as they had all made a pact with the devil who allowed them to cast their spells.

By the time they reached Newport, Rhode Island the crew was worked into a frenzy of fear and couldn't wait to get off the ship. Sam and Gamba immediately went to Paulsgrave and told him the story. There was nothing that Paulsgrave could do as the Wantons were elected officials and had not broken any laws. Sam's only option was to wait until the auction and legally purchase the Africans, which would use almost all his money if they went for the standard price.

Sam was despondent for a couple of days until Paulsgrave offered to help fund the next expedition as he felt a little guilty about arranging for Sam to meet and trust the Wantons. Sam got involved with planning the next wrecking venture and started going all around town to arrange for ships stores and supplies while Paulsgrave found a ship. It turns out that Gamba was not only a warrior but somewhat of a natural politician. As he walked through town, he smiled and was subservient to all he encountered except for the sailors he knew from the ship who he stared at fiercely with hatred.

Whenever a sailor got hurt on the docks, they blamed Gamba and physically feared him. The sailors spread the stories of the Africans who could walk on water, cast a spell to make Sam walk on water, cast spells to harm those who captured and enslaved his friends, swim with sharks and lead an army of the dead in search of sunken treasure.

By the time that the auction came up, no one wanted to bid on the demon Africans. To save face, Captain Wanton sold them to Sam at a very low price with the agreement that he would remove them from town as quickly as possible, keep them out of sight until they left and never allow them to return to New England.

Even though Sam was now more financially stable and had a good wrecking crew (including Baba and John Julian), Paulsgrave still wanted to be his partner and go along. He was excited about the prospect of Africans leading sharks and an army of the dead to facilitate the search for the lost Spanish treasure. Sam was never sure if Paulsgrave really believed all that but his spreading the story made the venture very popular.

Sam did nothing to dampen Paulsgrave's enthusiasm for this great adventure, as he knew he would enjoy his company. Many of the less superstitious sailors on the docks wanted to join the great adventure with the skilled and fearless Africans leading their supernatural assistants and sharks to speed up the search for buried treasure. Even the sailors from the first trip wanted to go again. They only requested that the Africans forgive them and allow them to come along. Since Sam was able to get ample crew, it was not necessary to include any from the first expedition who Sam would never trust a second time.

Everybody involved (except Sam) believed this was an adventure, which could not fail and that all involved would be wealthy. Sam did nothing to feed the rumors or convince the crew that the Africans were magic but everybody was ready to believe a really good story. Since they had only acquired a small sloop with eight guns, a crew of twelve plus Sam, Paulsgrave and the Africans was more than enough to safely man the ship.

Among the more unusual ships'-stores was rough-cut lumber and heavy rope which his partner never challenged and Sam never explained. Sailors of the era would also never question why the Captain brought anything on board so it was only the wrecking crew members who understood why the timber was necessary.

Recovering Riches from the Sea

Chapter 8
An Accidental Pirate

From Newport, the treasure expedition traveled south to Jamaica to recruit two more African divers. They then headed further south to the Miskito Coast where they met with Baba and John Julian in the Miskito village North of Bluefields. Baba was now a member of the tribe as he had been introduced by John Julian and had taken a Miskito woman as his wife. He was accepted into the tribe as a wise elder.

Baba let his friends know that his treasure hunting days were over as he now had everything he wanted in life including a family and his new tribe. As a friend to Sam, and John Julian, he would do everything in his power to help plan their mission and when they went to sea, he would do everything possible to protect anything they kept hidden on the Miskito Coast. He would protect the treasure left on land by the group just as John Julian and he had protected the treasure left behind by Sam on their first trip.

The group decided that everyone involved, including Indians, Africans, and New England sailors would have equal shares except that Sam and Paulsgrave would get five extra shares; Sam for being the leader and Paulsgrave for owning the ship. They also set aside one share for the tribe who was committed to providing food and supplies on a weekly basis. In matters related to treasure hunting, only the original group of decision makers including Sam, Paulsgrave, John Julian, Gamba, Simba and Shumba would have a vote. The hope was that they would reach all decisions by consensus and not by vote and they referred to this group as The Council.

Planning went well for their venture as the group developed a fairly simple plan by consensus. They had two more African Divers to work with Simba and Shumba. Gamba would act as a personal assistant to Sam and Baba would remain on shore to protect their assets. They would need a total of three canoes and enough Miskito Indians to join the Africans and man the canoes.

John Julian and Baba knew that very few of the Indians wanted or needed a job or wealth. However, many would join for the great adventure and, if allowed to free dive, they would work to find and recover the iron tools associated with the wrecks. Of course, wherever they found desirable iron tools to build their canoes, the treasure would be close by.

The Council decided the only way to reward the transient Indians was for two extra shares to be set aside and for John Julian and Baba to dispense it to those who were occasional workers at the end of the recovery operations. They would know who the workers were and know how to fairly reward them to keep the whole tribe happy.

Their method of operation had been developed by the Africans while in Newport, and Sam had acquired the additional timber, ropes and pulleys they would need to improve their wrecking operations. Simba, Shumba and Gamba were experienced wreckers and had been involved with really professional wrecking recoveries as done by the Spanish. They planned to use the timber to build a platform between two of the canoes.

The floating platform would not be assembled until divers working from the canoes found some evidence of treasure. Then the platform and pulleys were to be assembled where needed and anchored in place. A basket weighted by stones would be lowered to the bottom through the middle of the platform and the stones replaced with treasure. The divers would dive and return to the platform because it was more stable than the canoes. These changes allowed the divers to work for a longer period of time and not waste energy carrying silver plate or bars to the surface. The platform would be moved as needed.

The Council agreed that the operation should be secretive and very low profile. The Africans and Miskito Coast Indians would work the wreck and deposit their treasure on the East Cay where they would retreat to each night. The island had enough brush to make cooking fires. Cooks would stay on land to prepare a slow cooked stew based on heavily spiced salted meat and fresh fish and non-perishable provisions. At dusk, the treasure from the days work would be loaded in the extra canoe and everyone would head to East Cay for a hearty dinner and a good night's sleep leaving the floating platform behind.

The Indians had planned ahead as they were familiar with the small cays in the offshore Banks. They brought poles to make lean-to shelters and hammocks to sleep in. Their biggest problem was the crabs and snails that came out at night to dine would try to feast on anyone trying to sleep on the ground. The wrecking crew slept at night in the hammocks while the cooks collected live crabs to be added to the stew pot. The cooks then rested in the shade of the lean-to shelters during the day.

The overall plan was for the Indians and Africans to work the dive site gathering treasure while the small Newport sloop stayed at sea. All agreed that the small group with low profile canoes was unlikely to be noticed by any European Ships. Even if they were noticed, few Captains would waste time and risk their ships trying to learn what the Indians and Africans were doing inside the Serranilla Shoals.

As star-crossed as Sam's first wrecking expedition was, his second attempt was blessed. John Julian and the original Africans found the area where they located the treasure on the first expedition. The sea in the area was relatively calm for winter and while they were setting up the floating dive platform, the remaining Indians used the third canoe and started diving the area looking for tools.

They were not diving in pairs as the Africans were trained to do, nor were they particularly well organized in which direction they dove. But the wrecking crew was blessed with an almost continuous find of iron tools and old guns. With great discipline, the Africans started searching where they had left off on the previous trip and moved in the general direction of where the Miskito Indians had found the tools. They were mostly interested in large blocks of dark coral because, they knew that after 100 years, piles of silver plate and bars would be covered with coral and smaller objects like tools and guns would continue to move with the current and rough seas.

After laying off for a week, it was time for Sam to meet with Simba and John Julian at Beacon Cay. John Julian representing the Miskito Indians, told Sam how excited they were with finding small iron items from the wreck and many wanted the Africans to move the diving platform to their area to help them. The Africans wanted to stay where they were as they were convinced they were in the right area as they had recovered a few silver bars and some plate. They had brought the silver to the rendezvous on Bacon Cay and were insisting they continue diving where they were because that is where they had found the heavy bars which would not have been carried to the North with the current like smaller lighter tools.

Simba, Sam and John Julian came to an agreement that Sam would take the ship on a food run to the Miskito Coast and drop off the silver and tools and return with food and an extra canoe. In the two weeks it would take to return, everyone would continue diving in the area where they thought they might get the best reward.

Upon the return, they would reallocate their resources based on the results. If the results to the north were encouraging, they would leave two Africans with the diving platform and assign the other two African divers to the additional canoe in the expanded search area to improve their chance of finding the mother load of silver plate and bars.

The trip to the Miskito Coast and back was uneventful and upon returning Sam directed the ship to go to East Cay and they fired a small signal cannon several times until the cooks spotted them. The next evening, Simba Shumba and John Julian showed up and met with Sam on Beacon Cay. Their canoe was almost overloaded with Silver Plate and South American jewels and they had left even more on East Cay. It seems that Simba and Shumba had discovered part of the motherlode and everybody got so excited with the find that they all started working in harmony to bring the treasure to the surface.

The underwater treasure was almost endless. As they reached the end of one pile, it inevitably pointed them in the direction of the next pile. The divers were almost continuously diving to fill the basket and when the basket was full, the Miskito Indians would haul it to the surface while the divers took a break. They had been diving on the Treasure for almost six days and were not even close to being finished. At this point, the Miskito Indians began to understand that they would have more than enough European wealth to buy all the iron tools they would ever need and were losing interest in the venture because of the continuous hard work.

The wrecking crew had accumulated more wealth than Sam's small lightly armed sloop could safely carry. The Council decided (with Baba missing) that they should take the gems and cobs and hide them in the hidden compartments Sam had had his sailors build into the ship during their idle time. They would carry a bag of coins in the captains quarters to convince pirates they had already sold their trade goods and put as much silver bar as reasonable in the bottom of the hold with the dirtiest coral encrusted silver on top and then on top of that were a couple of rows of ballast bricks for additional camouflage.

[*Note: Cobs or macuquinas are the original "treasure coins." Struck and trimmed by hand in the 16th through 18th centuries at Spanish mints in Mexico, Peru, and Colombia (among others), silver and gold cobs are crudely made, nearly all with a cross as the central feature on one side and either a coat-of-arms (shield) or a tic-tac-toe-like "pillars and waves" on the other side. Some cobs after 1607 were struck with a date. Size and shape were immaterial as long as the assay and weight were correct. Subsequently, most cobs are far from round or uniform in thickness. Cobs were generally accepted as good currency all around the world, and were the coins pirates referred to as "pieces of eight" if silver, and "doubloons," if gold.*]

Once again all of the excess food and water were left with the Miskito Indians and Africans. When then reached the Serrana Shoals, they began to be stalked by two pirate ships working together, a small fast one and a slower heavily armed one. Sam ran from the ships for almost a week using his knowledge of the waters around the shoals to his advantage. Unfortunately, he had used up most of his food supplies and needed to acquire food and water for his own crew and the wrecking crew still working the Serranilla Shoals.

As with all desperate men in need of supplies, Bellamy and Williams intercepted a smaller sloop to obtain the supplies they were more than willing to pay for. They were forced to abandon the transaction when they were attacked by pirates Henry Jennings and Charles Vane who had a much larger force and had been the ones chasing them.

Jennings and Vane had no intention of robbing them and didn't even board the boat. All they wanted was a parley to discuss joining forces for the taking of a French frigate, which would require more help. They assumed Sam and his crew were pirates as they had stopped the smaller sloop and were armed. Since discretion is the better part of valor, Captain Bellamy and his group joined forces in early March, 1716 to take the French frigate.

So, after diving on the Serranilla shoals for a few weeks with great success, Sam's career as a pirate started as an accident.

Sam and his crew were instrumental in stopping the frigate and getting them to strike their colors. Sam had used his ship to get ahead of the frigate with Jennings and Vane behind it. As he passed ahead of it he had Gamba and the Indians line up along the side while Gamba gestured with his two cutlasses and the

Miskito Coast Indians were armed with their weapon of choice, European muskets. which had been provided to them by pirates and later the English government to fight the Spanish. Sam ordered that a shot be fired across the bow of the ship and he ordered the Captain of the frigate to strike his colors. Unbelievable to Sam and his company, the Captain complied. Sam held back and allowed the crews of Jennings and Vane to board the ship.

The entire crew of Captain Bellamy's ship stood in horror as they watched the senseless slaughter of the crew and civilians on deck leaving only a few sailors alive. Circumstances dictated that they stay with Jennings and Vane and assist in capturing additional ships. They allowed the two captains to board the ships and consented to whatever portion they received. Jennings and Vane never questioned their subservient actions but accepted the inferior position of Captain Bellamy as their just due.

This partnership was doomed to failure as Jennings and Vane were cruel and viscous pirates who were prone to acts of violence without cause or reason. Sam's luck held out as the rigging on his foresail tore out and he needed to go to a safe anchorage for repairs. Since they were in the vicinity of the Serrana Banks, Sam suggested he anchor behind the Southwest Cay in the safe anchorage. Jennings and Vane had never heard of this safe anchorage and joined Sam in sailing to the spot. Sam used his Miskito Coast Indians to guide him but Jennings and Vane just assumed that Sam was a very skilled navigator and captain.

When they reached the anchorage, Sam estimated that repairs would take about a week. The other Captains trusted Bellamy, who had been so subservient, that they decided to leave the French frigate behind and go in search of more treasure. Unknown to Jennings and Vane, Bellamy and Williams had an older back up sail they could quickly put in place instead of repairing the newer sail at this time.

They took this as a chance to break away and before leaving, Bellamy and Williams stole much of the wealth that had been taken from the French frigate and parted company.

Jennings and Vane returned in a rage as their trip had been unsuccessful and they had lost the wealth of the French Frigate. They brutally killed more than 20 French and English sailors of captured ships and burned a captured merchant sloop.

Vane never had the brains to either quit or succeed as a pirate. He was infamous for his cruelty toward the crews of captured vessels routinely torturing men on the ships he captured. He never honored the pirate's code or even his own word of honor. He killed sailors who surrendered and wanted to join him and cheated his own sailors out of their share - a severe violation of the pirate code. His actions on this occasion were consistent with his entire career.

After departing from Jennings and Vane, Williams and Bellamy diverted south to the Miskito Coast and the village of John Julian to check on the well being of the Wrecking Crew and also, to share their wealth with the Indians and divers. This loyalty to his crew was a fortunate decision. Jennings and Vane thought that Williams and Bellamy would run north to Jamaica to dispose of their wealth and took that course.

The wrecking crew had not finished their tasks but when fresh water got low, they knew they had to leave despite the abundance of food in the area. Since everyone was safely united on the Miskito Coast, The Council took time to safely plan their future with the ship laying off the Miskito Coast in the opposite direction of Jamaica.

The biggest problems they faced were they were not done mining the motherlode of wealth and at the same time everyone on board the ship was now considered a pirate of the worst sort as they had consorted with Jennings and Vane. For better or worse, there were few witnesses to this as they never boarded another ship and Jennings and Vane killed everyone they could not use to their advantage.

John Julian, the Africans and a few of the Indians wanted to enjoy life at sea as free men and pirates. The twelve Sailors who had been recruited in Rhode Island as treasure hunters were divided with about half wanting to return home and the rest wanting to stay at sea and continue the wrecking operations. Sam recognized he did not have enough wealth to marry Maria Hallett so he had no choice but to remain at sea.

His friend Paulsgrave was enjoying his new life of adventure and decided to remain with Sam. The Council collectively decided that those who did not want to continue a life at sea including piracy would be dropped in Jamaica to find their way home.

John Julian decided to leave his treasure on land because he had no need for it at sea. Sam and the rest of the crew decided to leave everything of value with the Miskito Coast Indians rather than being identified as pirates by their possessions. They decided they would return for the wealth when they had established a base of operations and were powerful enough to fear no men.

They still had unfinished work to do on the wrecking operation at the Serranilla Banks and there was still a fortune that had been recovered and left at the base of the large coral outcropping on Beacon Cay.

The Pirates made their way to Jamaica and took no other ships along the way. While Jamaica was no longer a pirate haven, no one officially cared so long as everybody behaved and no one came into port identifying them as pirates. Of course it became an open secret that this was the ship and the crew that had outsmarted Jennings and Vane.

Sam had no problem finding a trusted Leghorn Merchant to take the retiring farmer/sailors to Newport. The merchant assured him that the sailors and their wealth would arrive safely in Rhode Island. Before the ship left, Sam and Gamba met with the sailors and swore them all to secrecy about the exact site of the wrecking operation and told them to always refer to the site as the Serrana Banks. If they wanted to tell tall tales they had heard while at sea be unclear about locations. This was easy as none of the sailors had even seen the Africans and Miskito Indians working at the wrecking location or even knew the exact location. Also, it was only the Africans and Indians who were involved in hiding the treasure they had recovered on Beacon Cay before returning to the Miskito Coast.

Since they were leaving the group before the wrecking job was completed, all agreed that a half share of the recovered treasure was acceptable and The Council voted that Williams and Bellamy receive the extra portion, as they had been responsible for making everyone wealthy beyond their wildest dreams. The vote of The Council was dominated by John Julian and the African divers who had no great need for European wealth and barely understood what motivated Sam Bellamy and Paulsgrave Williams to fund the mission and endanger their lives. The Newport sailors left happy as they also got a full share of the treasure stolen from Jennings and Vane.

Sam also warned the retiring Newport sailors to never mention their short time as pirates as it would endanger their lives and the lives of the sailors left behind. They would also lose their fortunes as the profits of pirates belonged to the Crown while wreckers could keep some of their recovered treasure. Overall it was best to keep quiet about the amount of money they had. Gamba just stared at the sailors and put the fear of God and the Devil into them to insure they would keep their oath of silence.

Sam knew that he would have no trouble recruiting new sailors to be pirates. At the height of the War of Spanish Succession, there were 50,000 sailors in the Royal Navy. When the war ended, 37,000 sailors were dismissed with little money and no chance of finding work on land, as it would take a while to reopen factories and expand trade with the colonies. Some with farming backgrounds could return home but most would just be a further burden on their poor farming families. Those who returned to the cities would be lucky if they could get sent to jail for being on a post-war merchant ship was just like being in jail only with a chance of being drowned.

Merchant Captains were hated even more than the Royal Navy. One London merchant ship left London with a crew headed for the West Indies and back to Portugal and Italy before returning to London. The pay was 4 pounds per month. When the ship reached Lisbon, the Captain heard the war was over. He fired the crew and left them stranded. He hired a new crew at less than 1.5 pounds per month.

Upon reaching Livorno [Leghorn, Italy], the Captain again fired his crew and hired another one for even less. Because of conditions, there was an abundance of skilled sailors left over from the war who were more than willing to turn pirate and make war against merchants and governments, but Sam was looking for very special men to join his crew.

Sam was looking for men just like those who had manned the Newport sloop in his second wrecking expedition. He wanted men who would fight when necessary, become pirates to survive and were honest and loyal. He was essentially looking for God fearing, hard working farmers who only became sailors out of economic necessity. He knew he would make mistakes of character so he hired ten men at 4 pounds per month to replace the six he had lost and would put them immediately to the test.

When they got out to sea, he explained to the group that they would be involved in the continuation of a wrecking operation. The first part of their job would be to transport and protect the treasure previously discovered to the Miskito Coast. They would be paid sailors wages but not share equally in this wealth as that treasure was discovered and was owned by the remaining members of his wrecking crew.

The second part of the job was to support the continuing wrecking operation of the Africans and Miskito Coast Indians and they would get a share of any additional wealth recovered.

Sam started by going north and joining forces with known pirates as they were not strong enough to stand alone against Jennings and Vane. Once the got some associates and experience, they would go south to finish the wrecking operation. The crew of the Newport sloop now consisted of 6 Newport sailors, 4 Miskito Indians, the 2 newer African divers, John Julian, Gamba, Simba, Shumba, Sam, Paulsgrave and the 10 new sailors out of Jamaica. Thus, the loyal core group who had a lot to lose outnumbered the new members and Gamba was always on the watch protecting Sam.

Bellamy and Williams joined forces with Benjamin Hornigold in late March 1716, to learn how to battle pirates. Despite violating the Pirate Code by running off with the treasure of Jennings and Vane, the Pirates in the Hornigold fleet decided to accept them as consorts because of all the people Vane had cheated in the past.

Hornigold was not only a legendary pirate, but also a mentor and leader of other pirates including Edward Teach who would gain great fame under the name Blackbeard. Olivier Levasseur, also known as Olivier La Buse, was loosely affiliated with the group. On some occasions he cooperated with Hornigold and on some occasions, he worked independently.

Olivier Levasseur and Sam became fast friends and while they sailed looking for a ship to take, they often sailed together and talked. He was honest with La Buse and told him about the wrecking expedition and the need to protect himself from pirates. Olivier suggested Sam fly a black flag which would keep most honest pirates away and that he get a bigger gun to keep any aggressive pirates at bay. He had to have one well-trained gunner for the 12 pound cannon and he had to be diligent that no one be allowed to approach his ship without his permission. As to Jennings and Vane, he should never allow them close to his ship under any circumstances because you could not trust their word or a request to parley.

The first ship that they all took of their own free will as pirates was a slow moving Bristol Ship south of Pettyguavus [Petit-Goave, Haiti] heading for Jamaica. The ship had sold its cargo of slaves in the Windward Islands and only had cash and a few passengers heading to Jamaica. Sam had schooled his crew that senseless violence was a wasted effort and all of the sailors were in the same shape as they were and they should not harm fellow poor people unless absolutely necessary, but like Robin Hood's Men, they should rob from the rich and share with the poor while keeping some for themselves.

The taking of the ship was easy. He had his best gunner manning the 12-pounder as he passed the slave ship and he had dummies manning all of the other cannons, just as Captain Morgan had done in his great escape from Lake Maracaibo. Sam had Gamba and the Africans waving their cutlasses over their heads; John Julian and the Miskito Coast Indians waved their guns; and the sailors waved cutlasses and pistols.

All it took was one shot across the bow from the 12-pound cannon and Sam's order to strike their colors and the Bristol ship capitulated. Sam and a party of five boarded the ship as the remaining sailors manned the cannons. La Buse moved up on the other side with his larger force of men.

Sam explained to the Captain he could work with him or he and his small crew would leave the ship and abandon him to the larger force of French pirates who had little use for the English. The Captain took the message to heart and handed Sam his purse. Sam took about ¾ and left the Captain enough to start over. He then handed 2 pounds to each sailor on board the slaver and every new sailor on his own ship. He then gave the rest to La Buse because money was not a real issue to him or his original crew. A few of the sailors from the captured ship wanted to join him but Sam had all the manpower he needed to support the wrecking operation.

The robbing of the ship was so easy because of Sam's knowledge of Merchant Trade. He knew roughly the number of slaves on board and the value of a slave in the Eastern Caribbean so if the Captain had lied, Sam would have known and turned the ship over to the French to tear it apart and torture the Captain until they found the money. Once the Captain realized this, he capitulated.

During the month of April, the Newport sloop moved south and was used exclusively to support the Wrecking Expedition. The operation was far more efficient as Sam stopped ships at will and dealt with the Captains. All he asked was a steady source of food, water, supplies and secrecy. If they failed him, he would sink their ship with all hands on board. He also recognized the larceny in most men's hearts so he traded old Spanish silver bars and plate for new silver cogs at a discount and an even greater discount for gold doubloons. Sam wanted the most compact source of common currency to carry back to New England when it was time.

Their regular route was an area around the Serrana Banks and off the coast of Nicaragua to gather provisions especially water, then carry the food and water to the wreckers. On the return leg they took the silver bar stock with them to trade with captains for new coins.

Sam's principle trading partners were the merchants from the Dutch West Indies Trading Company who had enough capital to take advantage of the discounts. In addition, the Dutch East Indies Trading Company needed silver to use for the coins they minted so the Dutch of the West Indies involved in the slave trade had the capital to purchase the silver in the West Indies and a market to sell the silver for a profit in Holland.

The Wrecking Expedition finished up in about six weeks and the Newport sloop made several trips to the Miskito Coast from the Serranilla Shoals to store their accumulated wealth. It was now time for Sam to head north and catch up with Hornigold and La Buse as he now had a desperate need for a ship large enough to carry his fortune back to Cape Cod and take his rightful place in society.

Meanwhile from May to June, 1716, La Buse and Hornigold had been cruising the Caribbean in the vicinity of Hispaniola while using a sheltered bay with access to fresh water know to La Buse. Hornigold still refused to attack British ships and that limited the success of the pirates. His ship, the Benjamin, was in desperate need of repairs. To get repairs and to get some needed cash for his crew, he took all the trade goods and headed to the Bahamas where there were safer ports for pirates.

When Sam arrived in late June, Hornigold was gone so he joined forces with La Buse in the heavily armed Postillion and they continued to cruise the area around Hispaniola without limiting themselves to non-British ships.

In the Month of June 1716, Captain John Brett was taken by Capt. Samuel Bellamy in his Newport sloop with his partner Captain La Buse in his sloop, the Postillion. After talking with the Captain of the ship and getting nowhere, Sam turned him over to La Buse for his sailors to search the ship. After thoroughly searching the ship and finding nothing, they damned the pathetic ship for sinking and told the Captain to bring his liquor on board. They carried the captain and his crew to the Isle of Pynes, where La Buse detained them as prisoners for eighteen days in hopes of getting a ransom.

It was during this time that the crew of the Newport sloop first learned of the harsher side of piracy. John Brown, who was active on board La Buse's Sloop told a prisoner that he would hide him in the hold and hinder him from complaining against him or telling his side to a story of cruelty. He also told the prisoner that he would have no more problem shooting him in the head than he would a dog. This was to be a fairly common threat by John Brown.

Bellamy in command of the Newport sloop and La Buse aboard the Postillion took another ship in July before the return of Hornigold and the sailors of the Newport sloop got to observe more of pirates' mindless terrorism.

When they stopped their next ship all they could take was provisions as there was no money or trade goods and the cash on hand was a pittance. Some of the Dutch pirates aboard the Postillion lingered on board and questioned Capt. Thomas Fox about whether any harm had come to the pirates in the Boston jail. When Captain Fox legitimately answered he knew nothing about them, one Dutchman belonging to La Buse questioned Fox further about a particular Dutch man in the Boston Goal and said that if the prisoners suffered, they would kill every New

England sailors they captured in the future.

Sam's wrecking crew was discovering the true world of piracy and protesting to Sam about the senseless violence. Meanwhile, Hornigold was having his own problems. Upon his return, Hornigold was trying to discipline and reprimand Bellamy and La Buse for taking British ships while he has gone. Unfortunately for Hornigold, all of the English pirates on his ships became involved in the discussion.

Because Hornigold refused to take and plunder English Vessels, Sam Bellamy was chosen by a great majority as their Captain, and Hornigold departed with 26 hands in the recently acquired Adventure while Bellamy then had on board the Marianne, about 90 men, most of them English. Since Williams was the actual owner of the Newport sloop, the pirates agreed he should keep it and the wrecking crew voted to sail with Captain Paul Williams.

After the split, La Buse convinced Sam and his crew that their group needed a safe harbor where they could repair their ships, gather supplies, get food and water and defend themselves against French and English Naval attacks and rogue pirates like Vane. La Buse convinced Sam and the English Pirates that St. Croix would be the perfect pirate haven and, at the end of August, the three ships headed for St. Croix.

Along the way to St. Croix, the crew of the Marianne insisted on using their newly acquired Democracy to make all decisions. Instead of listening to Sam's logic of searching for rich merchant ships and limiting the number of new volunteers, the crew voted on all issues and insisted on stopping every small fishing vessel they came in contact with and allowing every deckhand who wanted to be a pirate to join them.

Deck hands are not sailors, but men known for their strong backs and equally weak minds. They draw in the nets and pull up fish traps while the sailors man the boat.

As result, the crew grew in number with more mouths to feed and no additional rewards to pay the additional crew. Fortunately, La Buse and his disciplined crew stopped a French merchant carrying flour and salted cod, took enough to feed the entire fleet and let the merchant ship go.

Père Jean-Baptiste Labat

Chapter 9
Water, Fuel, Meat, Provisions and Fruit

Olivier Levasseur promised Sam that the island of St. Croix was a tropical paradise. There was no official government so it could be run like a pirate republic using the standard pirate contracts or articles and there was everything a pirate needed to get a ship ready for battle.

There was pork, beef, fowl, fish and fruit in abundance. There was enough wood and water to supply an infinite number of ships and it was centrally located to attack Spanish ships to the south and English ships to the north and east.

Olivier explained to Sam before they left for St. Croix that his information on the island was extremely accurate and at one point the information had been a military secret.

French privateers had used the island during the War of Spanish Succession and the British never discovered their activity and treated it like an unoccupied island not worth the bother to explore during the war. Even better, during the current peace, the English had to respect French sovereignty regardless of any suspicions they might develop.

There were two sheltered and somewhat hidden ports on the North side of the island and a somewhat hidden anchorage in the middle of the south side of the island. The military assessment had been completed and the importance of the island was described privately to the King just as the War of Spanish Succession started. It became general knowledge among French privateers during the war as all of them used it to repair their ships and replenish supplies.

It seems that prior to the death of Charles II of Spain, everybody in power in France accepted there would be a war over dominance in Europe.

Since Spain was no longer a military power, France would be forced to fight most of Europe alone. Thus, France started gathering military intelligence before King Charles II had resigned and subsequently died.

[Authors Note: From 1690 to 1700, Europe was in turmoil.

Because of the Divine Right of Kings and hereditary succession, the people of Spain accepted that God had given them Charles II. He had been King since he was 3 years old despite the fact he had severely retarded physical, mental and emotional development. There was no way to politely describe this handicapped King. He was ignored by all his ministers who governed as they wished. He finally died in November 1700.

Charles II had no heir of his own so his will left his kingdom to a French relative who was also heir to the French throne thus creating the potential for a joint Monarch for France and Spain. To block the potential for the joint monarchy, the War of the Spanish Succession broke out shortly after his death.]

The military assessment of the Caribbean had been carried out by Jean-Baptiste Labat, a French clergyman, botanist, writer, explorer, soldier, engineer, and landowner. In his earlier years, besides preaching, he taught philosophy and mathematics. After moving to the Caribbean, he owned slaves and plantations while focusing on improving the sugar cane production process for all Frenchmen.

Because of his broad scientific knowledge, the French

government appointed him as an engineer. In this capacity, he visited the French, Dutch, and English Antilles from Grenada to Hispaniola gathering information wherever he went. On his way to Saint-Domingue (Haiti) , he stopped at St. Croix to explore the island and gather meat and fruit for the ship.

There is little doubt that this was a military mission and he was in charge. As the following diary information indicates he stayed as long as he wanted to explore St. Croix and was accompanied by three pirates. He constantly ignored the captain of the ship and gathered the information presented below at his leisure.

Pirates and privateers rarely kept written records for fear of being hung and the complete diary of Labat was not published until 1742, well after both he and the French King (Luis XIV) he criticizes are both dead. When it was published, the Golden Age of Piracy was over and Denmark owned the Island of St. Croix.

From the diary of Labat:

The currents then carried us so close to St. Croix, that we were obliged to anchor. We were at Salt River Bay, with the main capital of the old colony, about half a league away [1.5 miles]. I asked our captain to lend us his lifeboat to go look for fresh meat. He graciously did.

I took our two Negroes with me. Three of our passengers, who were the Pirates of Santo Domingo, boarded with four Sailors & a Pilot. We had good weapons & provision including bread & wine. Father Cabasson knowing that we would sleep on the ground threw my hammock to me as we passed around the vessel.

We entered Salt River Bay about a mile inland and sat down on the ground at the walls of a Sugar factory that might have been restored inexpensively. After our lifeboat moored, we left one of the Sailors & an armed Negro behind to make a gazebo & fire.

We began to hunt and first slayed a calf about six months old with full fat skin. His mother, who was not happy, came in with head down and was killed by our company. We dressed the calf in the field. As to the Ship, we sent half of the calf to our Captain to celebrate and so he would be able to listen to reason.

The rowboat returned with a fifth Seaman & two passengers, and Father Cabasson asked me to return the next day at dawn.

I never found myself more abundant hunting; The Park at Versailles in France was nothing in comparison.

We killed in less than a league of our camp seven thick boars & much piglets; We also killed common cocks & hens which had become wild, pigeons, and other fowl, as much as we wanted. We made a great fire, a great boucan, and were merry all night. And the fun we had scarcely allowed us to sleep, to which must be added that the unwelcome company of mosquito & swamp mosquitoes did wonders to keep us awake. I managed a few hours of sleep in my hammock all bundled up.

Early in the day our captain fired a Canon Appelier for us to board. We replied with nine or ten shots, and we sent the lifeboat led by three Pirates & our two Negroes with meat, with orders to tell him to do noise making (cannon fire) as we gathered provision for her voyage.

As we did, all went flat calm.

Father Cabasson came to spend the day with us. We visited the sad remains of our Establishment. The thickets (bushes and vines) already covered almost every wall. In truth, it is a horrible thing to have destroyed a beautiful colony for a vile [political] interest, and to have reduced to beggary many good inhabitants who were well accommodated in this island with abundant fresh water *reserves, a rare commodity in many places.*

We observed a lovely place. This is an almost flat island: there are only hills, or to speak the language of the islands, there are the hills towards the middle of the Island, the slopes are gentle, they are covered with the most beautiful trees in the world. The Mahogany, the wood of India, the Acoma, the Balatas, red wood there are all strong in abundance. We even saw some beautiful Cannes [sugar cane] despite the ravages pigs & other livestock did to it.

There are Oranges & lemon trees of quantity. We have found Cassava, and excellent potatoes. We saw the sea on the other side of the island from all the hills where we went, which made me conjectured that there scarcely will be three leagues of coast to coast in the place where we were. We are told that it was one of the narrowest parts of the islands. [Who told them?]

Father Cabasson went back to sleep on board. The next morning the driver told us that there was appearance of wind. We had lunch & returned to the vessel loaded with fat meat, game & fruit, more than we could eat in 15 days. The wind got up as the afternoon progressed, we weighed anchor, and ran torward our destination."

The passage above is from: "*Labat, Jean-Baptiste, 1663-1738. Nouveau voyage aux isles de l'Amérique Chapter 2, Vol. 7. Paris : Ch. J.B. Delespine. Published 2d ed., 8 vols., 1742*" While all this was general knowledge to the French Military, it was not published until much later so Sam had to put a lot of faith in his fellow Captain Olivier Levasseur to make St. Croix his home.

Sam Bellamy was happy with what he found when he arrived on the island of St. Croix. Indeed it was an ideal place to build his pirate republic with ample food, wood and water. Shelter could be easily rebuilt.

Fortification of the Port at St. Croix

Chapter 10

People to Work the Land

The biggest surprise when Sam reached the island was the number of English settlers as he expected an abandoned island.

In January 1696, all planters on St. Croix were moved to Haiti along with their families, livestock and slaves. While depopulated by the French Crown, the island was not abandoned. The French maintained possession by occasional military operations and the French did not officially transfer it to the Danish until 1733. During the whole of the Golden Age of Piracy, there were no official Government Administrators from any Nation in charge of the island.

After the French abandoned the island, there were occasional poor English squatters who came to the island to cut wood because they could not earn a living on the English Islands as planters. In 1699, Louis XIV gave specific orders to remove any squatters from the island and settle the French Citizens on French Colonies and drop the others at St. Thomas.

Apparently these orders were not consistently enforced. By the time the French transferred the island to the Danish, the population of this secret colony had grown to 150 Englishman and 456 slaves or about half the size of the French Colony of St. Croix in 1695 when the French moved everyone to Haiti.

Not only had the island population recovered but it would appear, the planters were more prosperous as the ratio of slave to white on the English plantations was a little above three slaves to one white and on the

French plantations in 1695, the ratio had been about half that level.

Sam found out that the increased population of St. Croix was a direct result of the visit by Jean-Baptiste Labat. He had made contact with the English squatters who were largely religious dissenters not fond of the English Monarchy or Church of England.

Being a military man, Labat offered a pragmatic solution. The squatters could stay under the condition that they operate as suppliers and ships' chandlers, gathering and supplying everything the French privateers might need. If they did their jobs well, they could stay and be paid for their efforts.

Obviously, secrecy was necessary for the French privateers and pirates as well as the English squatters. If the English wanted to go, they could, but if they stayed, they had to be well hidden because the British would consider them traitors and hang them. Most stayed and more joined them as the need arose. The port also acted as a free port where merchants could buy and privateers could sell trade goods without taxation or manifests.

The ships needed fresh water, food, and firewood. Water and wood are heavy and food goes bad. So the shorter time between replenishing supplies, the better for everyone on board the ship.

After the creation of the pirate republic, it was fairly common knowledge that St. Croix was a port for duty free transactions and obtaining supplies. In 1724, Charles Johnson wrote his book "*A GENERAL HISTORY OF THE PYRATES,*" which has never been out of print from that time.

In this book, Johnson mentions St. Croix in reference

to pirate activity nine times with some extremely creative spellings. In his chapter on the destruction of the James Martel pirate gang, there is an episode at the end of 1716, where Captain Hume was investigating a report of Pirates around the British Virgin Islands.

Since he found none he was ready to return at sunrise to his base in Barbados. However, "that Night [January 16, 1717], ... *a Boat [arrived] there [the British Virgin Islands] from Santa Cruz, and informed him, that he saw a Pyrate Ship of 22 or 24 Guns, with other Vessels, going in to the North West Part of the Island.*"

There was no English objection with legitimate merchant ships dealing with the Englishmen on St. Croix so a report to officials could be honestly made about pirate activity without fear of recriminations.

The Christiansted port was well defended by four gun placements and everyone entered the free port under a flag of truce to do their business. The British, Dutch and Jewish Merchants had no problem dealing with the people of St. Croix and the only ones who were disturbed were the French Military. Olivier Levasseur did his best to smooth everything over and to make sure that the French Captains got their needed supplies. However, there was little they could do about the secret colony.

The main part of the French fleet was in Haiti and to return to St. Croix against the wind and current was more than a little difficult. So long as no French ships were attacked in the area, pirates were allowed to stay. This was an easy promise to keep because there were not many French ships that used the routes near St. Croix on a regular basis. Moreover, many of the

French captains approved of privateers particularly against English ships.

The isolated location also gave minimum protection from the Royal Navy. British merchant ships usually did line of sight sailing along the island chain until they reached St. Thomas before heading to Jamaica. In this way merchant ships had the protection of Forts on the British Islands they passed and any pirate foolish enough to operate in sight of a British Island was asking for retribution because the Royal Navy would seek to crush them just as Captain Hume would do to James Martel in Salt Rive Bay.

The longer they stayed on St Croix, the more problems Sam was having in controlling his new crew. Decisions on board the ship were becoming more violent and irrational the longer they stayed on St. Croix and his partner, Olivier Levasseur, was not experiencing the same problem.

As they discussed the problem, Sam came to understand more about the difference between French and English pirates. The French pirates were mostly Huguenots, originally from the Normandy District of France who were professional seamen with wives and children at home. The longer they earned a living at sea, the more they could send home to their families and the better the retirement they would have. Whenever French pirates wanted to return to their wives, there were always Huguenot sailors to replace them.

Olivier Levasseur was clearly of aristocratic birth and all his sailors recognized it. The ship was his and the men worked for a share of the prize. The men had a say but in the end, he made the best decisions for the common good. La Buse, as he was called, believed in the equality of men as there were no slaves in France. Also, since he was no longer particularly religious, he believed there were no inferior or superior religions and nothing to fight about. The job of his men at sea was to make as much money as possible with the least risk to sailors and their ship.

Sam's original wrecking crew on board the Newport sloop had a similar organizational structure. Williams owned the sloop, Sam was the Captain and all the sailors were hired help who would share in any recovered treasure. Sam made his decisions in consultation with the members of the Council on board the ship.

When they separated from Benjamin Hornigold, because of his restriction of taking British ships, the crew members of the Newport sloop and the crew of La Buse had the same goal; that is, they wanted to make enough money to have a comfortable life for them and their future families. The crew on the Marianne, was different. They were pirates who lived for the moment and when they thought about their situation at all, they recognized they had no future.

Careening a Ship

Chapter 11

Surrounded by a Few Good Men & then there were none

As the pirate partners sailed to St. Croix to start a new stage of their lives, Sam had reflected on the events that made him captain of a pirate ship. Since his initial encounter with pirates Henry Jennings and Charles Vane, he also begun to reflect on the type of men who became pirates.

There were unusual cases like his partners, Olivier Levasseur AKA Olivier La Buse ("Olivier the Buzzard") and Paulsgrave Williams who seemed to participate in piracy as a test of skill and mental competence or from a sense of adventure. He did not see himself in their class but classified himself as being similar to the French Huguenot pirates. Of course he wanted to be rich enough to marry the woman of his dreams, Maria Hallett, but he also thought of himself as a religious dissenter in a fight with an unjust King.

Among the pirates who served as ordinary seamen, he had noticed two types. The first group could be classified as criminals without a conscience. These brutal men terrorized the high seas and achieved their modest success by excessive force and terror.

Some of these criminals got elected and served as Captain using the same tactics. Jennings and Vane were typical criminals without consciences who engaged in terror just because they could do it and get away with it. They were village bullies who never grew up. If piracy did not exist, they would be terrorizing the streets of London and the streets of other large cities.

The other group he clearly identified was farmers running from famine. The problem with small scale farming in England was there was more farm labor than needed during periods of excessive drought or heavy rains. The land was owned by Gentleman who usually leased it to Tenant Farmers who managed the farm and hired commoners when there was work to do.

During periods of famine prices for produce rose but there was only limited work available to the commoners so they could not even afford the food they helped produce in the countryside. Some moved to the cities for industrial jobs or turned to a life of crime. Others took to the sea on the merchant ships, which paid seasoned sailors poorly and had extremely low wages for novice sailors.

The best a new sailor could hope for on board a merchant ship was better food then starving to death in England during times of famine. During times of war, the experienced sailors would land a place in the English Navy where both the food and wages were better and much better than starving on a farm. When peace came and the Navy was reduced in size, those who were let go would be forced to accept low wages on Merchant ships or return to farm labor and face periods of starvation.

Under these social and economic conditions, very few merchant sailors were willing to fight against pirates for fear of retribution if the pirates won, and many sailors on the worst merchant ships were willing to join the pirates in hopes for a better life.

As they sailed towards St. Croix, the sailors of Sam's wrecking crew shared the same goals of retiring rich as the French sailors did but had no way to execute the plan. They were not free to return to any British colonies, as the source of their wealth would be questioned just as severely as if they returned to the British Isles. This situation completely changed when they reached St. Croix.

La Buse explained to the islanders that the pirates were making La Bassin their home-port and that everything would be honored as it was by the privateers during the War of Spanish Succession. They would be paid for whatever goods or services they provided at reasonable prices. The pirates would secure the harbor with four cannon locations and make it impenetrable except for the most resolute enemy.

The crew on the Newport sloop was assigned to securing the harbor. They would recruit the settlers on the island who wanted to serve as militia men. Pirates were vulnerable when careening their ships or at anchorage in the harbor. Therefore, all able-bodied sailors in port would take turns manning the forts and gun emplacements during these periods.

Both Sam and La Buse explained to the people that it was in their best self-interest to join the pirates' Militia and support their existing status. They would all be paid for the time they spent training and manning the fort.

The Community would be governed by a modified Pirate Code which did not include a right to vote on issues but did have severe prohibitions against theft or fighting and killing each other or pirates doing them any harm. The importance of the Pirate Code, also called the Articles of Agreement, is because it is the first contractual Bill of Rights for commoners and seamen.

The Pirate Code developed by La Buse and Bellamy proves that all pirates were not depraved. About half of all surviving codes address the issue of women in a favorable manner. These codes warn that any man found seducing a woman and carrying her to sea disguised as a man, shall suffer death. This was a fairly common prohibition among pirates. Another part of the Bellamy code prohibited rape with a strong admonition; "If at any time you meet with a prudent woman, the man that chooses to meddle with her, without her consent, shall suffer death."

La Buse had been using St. Croix, ever since the war was over and he refused to give up privateering and return to France. There was a small but thriving community of people to serve his crew when he was visiting. There were two popular taverns and several establishments in town that served food.

The most popular drinking establishment was simply called Patty's Place. Patricia Latreille was an attractive full figured woman who was born on St. Croix in 1695, the year, that the French moved everyone to Haiti. Like most people from St. Croix, her parents got very poor land in Haiti and lived a miserable life. She left for the city of Cap-Haïtien when she was 16 years old to earn a better living. Cap-Haïtien was the capital of the French Colony of Saint-Domingue [Haiti] from the city's formal founding in 1711.

The capital city was bustling with visitors and she easily found work at a guest-house because of her vivacious personality. The owners were very religious and worked hard to keep her virtue in tact. She would flirt with and tease single male visitors. Everyone loved her company but still respected her virtues.

During the War of Spanish Succession, she met the very successful French Privateer Olivier Levasseur who convinced her she should move to St. Croix to start her own tavern.

Her tavern was a resounding success and she eventually learned English from her English patrons. Since everyone thought she was the girlfriend of La Buse, the men and visiting sailors left her alone. The only one in St. Croix that didn't like her was the owner of Lynn's Lair Tavern who was jealous of her success and popularity that she could never match.

After the war, Lynn started to fail from the loss of customers while Patricia continued to prosper. Finally, in the Fall of 1716, when the pirates of Bellamy and La Buse came to stay, there was enough business for both of them but the animosity continued for no reason at all and Patricia had no way to stop it.

After the arrival of the fleet of Bellamy and La Buse, the sailors seemed to gravitate to one of the two taverns based on the ship they were on or where their captain went. La Buse and all of the sailors of the Postillion tended to go to Patty's Pace as did Paul Williams and the Wrecking crew of the Newport sloop. Sam Bellamy accompanied by his friends John Julian and Gamba also frequented Patty's Place.

The cruder pirates that had voted Sam captain of the Marianne went to Lynn's Lair where they could engage in rougher entertainment of drinking, gambling, insulting each other and fighting without worrying about being disciplined by the captain or the quartermaster. So long as no one engaged in murder or rape, there was never an official sanction as no one complained to the captain or quartermaster.

There was never a charge of rape as the women who

frequented Lynn's Lair knew the type of men who were there and what was expected of them. The women were well rewarded as drunken sailors were notoriously loose with their money and paid for what they wanted.

The first person with the fleet that decided to settle on St. Croix was not a pirate at all. Tommy had been a passenger on a ship heading to North Carolina when his ship was intercepted by Hornigold who was looking for a few men to add to his ship's company. Tommy protested that he was not a sailor and would be of no use. He told them he was a tailor and that was his first big mistake, as Hornigold needed somebody to mend sails and make his pirate flags so he pressed Tommy into service.

Tommy did his job and more. He helped sailors mend their clothes and after one sailor got cut while working, he stitched up his wound. Tommy was a drinking man and made friends with everyone. He instinctively knew he should give a sailor as much alcohol as he wanted prior to trying to stitch him up.

As a tailor he had learned to be neat and clean. If he tried to sew clothes when dirty, he might soil a brand new garment so he kept himself meticulously clean. Also, he knew that stitching two pieces of jagged cloth together would never hold so he trimmed loose threads when sewing two pieces of cloth together. When he had to sew up a shipmate he followed these same procedures by staying clean and cutting off jagged flesh that would interfere with a smooth seam. After a while, his shipmates thought he had a magic touch as they seemed to heal faster, have fewer infections and his stitching always held until the healing was done. Unfortunately, this was his second mistake because he became indispensable to the pirates on the ship and the pirates swore they would never free him.

Still, Tommy never took a cent for his efforts even when generous pirates tried to pay him for saving their lives. He not only refused their ill gotten gains, he also refused to sign the pirate code and refused to tell anyone his last name in case he could jump ship or be rescued. The crew voted to let him get away with his protests because he was so cooperative and valuable otherwise and they just took to calling him "Tommy Tailor" and became friends with him.

When the fleet reached St. Croix, Tommy started working on getting more freedom from being at sea. He asked permission from Captain Bellamy to set up a tailor shop in town. He explained he would be far more efficient if he had a large place to work on sail making and repairs and he would still be available to patch old pirate clothes or fit new ones. He still did all the work for the pirates for free but he now had a few paying customers among the island settlers. Initially, he went to sea whenever Captain Bellamy took the Marianne in search of a larger ship that he could make into his man o' war to return to Boston with the treasure he had accumulated.

When Captain Bellamy captured the Sultana in September of 1716, he brought it to St. Croix to be converted to a man o' war. This was a major reconstruction as the ship had to be reinforced for a larger number of guns and accommodations created for a greater number of sailors on board. Sam also wanted some hidden compartments to hold cash on board in case they had to bribe a governor to look the other way. Because of a lack of skilled carpenters, work went slowly and Sam decided that they should use their spare time careening the boat for greater speed by removing the barnacles and coating the bottom with tar and sulfur.

The tar made a smooth surface for greater speed and bound the sulfur to the hull and the sulfur slowed down the regrowth of new barnacle colonies. Captain Bellamy went to sea in search of a carpenter on the Marianne. Meanwhile, Tommy Tailor stayed in port making new sails and repairing the old ones to be used for back-up when the man o' war finally went to sea.

During this time Tommy became friends with the Newport sailors while Bellamy and Williams used the Marianne to get the supplies they would need, particularly the tar, sulfur and cloth for new sails. The sailors quickly figured out that Tommy had very little money because he was neither a Pirate nor a wrecker. Since they all liked his company and had ample money from their time as wreckers, they paid for Tommy to join them. When Patty heard the story, she let Tommy work off his tab by making her place look better with curtains and oversize table clothes that doubled as napkins.

Over time, Tommy and Patty became the best of friends and he decided that he wanted to stay with her on St. Croix. He approached Captain Bellamy who was not a fan of forced labor but also would hate to lose a man who was a good tailor and a better surgeon than most. So Sam took the easy way out and said he would ask the company for their consent. He asked his company if they were willing to let Tommy go and got the answer he expected. They damned him and swore that they would slowly whip him to death at the mast with every pirate in the company taking a turn.

Tommy thought his dream was all over but Patty

decided that she couldn't work while worried about her Tommy so she shut her tavern down and forced everybody to go to Lynn's Lair. Almost immediately, Lynn had a ball stirring up trouble by spreading false rumors and telling lies about what the French sailors had said about the English. When fights started breaking out between the English on the Marianne and the French on the Postillion who had been enemies in the prior war, La Buse and Bellamy forced the shutting down of Lynn's Laird until Patty's Place reopened. When Patty was told, she replied she would reopen when Tommy was a free man and allowed to stay on St. Croix.

It came to pass fairly quickly that Tommy was given his freedom from the company and things returned to normal. Tommy continued to work for the pirates for free and the only pay he would allow was for the men to buy him dinner and drinks. As time passed, and after a little grumbling and several nights of drinking, past friendships were rebuilt. Lynn's Laird was firmly reestablished as the rowdy tavern where the pirates of the Marianne felt most comfortable.

In late October, Bellamy went to sea in the Marianne looking for a competent carpenter to speed up the rebuilding of the Sultana which had been proceeding very slowly for lack of a skilled master carpenter.

On November 9, 1716, operating from the Marianne off the coast of St. Croix, Bellamy and his crew captured the Antiguan sloop Bonetta under Captain Abijah Savage, which was traveling from Antigua to Jamaica. John King, then about eight years old was traveling with his mother and was to become the youngest pirate ever documented. [Note: According to a deposition from Abijah Savage, Captain of the Bonetta, King demanded to join Bellamy's crew and threatened to kill himself or harm his mother if he were not allowed to join. "Far from being forced or compelled to join he declared he would kill himself if he was restrained, and even threatened his Mother, who was then on board as a passenger..."]

Sam Bellamy initially wanted nothing to do with John King but was eventually swayed by the other pirates who refused to leave the ship and continued looting it for fifteen days while insisting King be allowed to join the company. Bellamy consented to John King becoming a pirate just so they could all get back to work and search for a master carpenter to finish the Sultana.

After releasing the Bonetta, they sailed towards the eastern Caribbean without much luck stopping smaller ships along the way to replenish their supplies. In early December, they once again joined forces with La Buse still not having found a carpenter. In mid December they got lucky and intercepted the Ship St. Michael commanded by Captain James Williams.

Captain Bellamy on the Marianne and Captain La Buse on the Postillion took the ship and found who they were looking for in carpenter, Thomas Davis, out of Bristol who was a single man. They took Davis and three other sailors along with the ship's provisions and released the St. Michael back to Captain Williams.

Captain Williams, protested the taking of the very young carpenter from Bristol to no avail. However, he did extract a promise from Captain Bellamy to release Davis to the next ship they took. [Note: The account by Sam was consistent with the testimony at the Trial of Thomas Davis as the pirates were described as operating from "two Pyrate Sloops, One Commanded by Capt Samuel Bellame, and the other by Monsr.

Memoirs of Captain Samuel Bellamy: 147

Louis La Bous." Most contemporary accounts have Bellamy in the Sultana at this time but that probably is not correct because mariners of that era could certainly be able to tell the difference between a galley and a sloop. The Marianne was a sloop while the Sultana was a galley similar to the HMS Bedford Galley. A galley was good for close in fighting if there was enough manpower on board to man the ores and additional manpower on deck to board the ship being attacked.]

The next stop was to Blanco Island (East of St. John) where they marooned the three men with ample provisions and water. At this point in late December, La Buse and Captain Bellamy went their separate ways and some pirates from La Buse's ship who wanted to join Bellamy on his man o' war were left to guard their future shipmates until Sam returned with the Sultana.

The sailors who were guards were: John Brown, born in Jamaica; Hendrick Quintor and Thomas Baker, both born in Holland; Peter Cornelius Hoof, born in Sweden (but the name is Dutch) and a Frenchman born in the French port of Le Havre on the Normandy Coast who everybody called Frenchie. They were all good brave fighters from the Postillion but would not initially be of much use as sailors because of their limited English (except for Brown). Captain Bellamy then returned to St. Croix to have Thomas Davis finish building the Sultana.

Captain Bellamy dropped off Thomas Davis with instructions to finish his man o' war and immediately went to sea and stopped every boat they passed from sailing dingies to larger sloops. He needed more manpower to man both the Sultana and Marianne and was looking for volunteers who wanted to be pirates.

Also his crew was looking for everything valuable they could find, not being aware of Sam's vast wealth still stored at the Miskito Coast. He dropped fourteen more willing men at Blanco Island and returned to St. Croix to put the Sultana to a sea test. Sam and his crew arrived at St Croix before Christmas at about the same time as Captain La Buse.

Upon arrival, he learned that with only Tommy Tailor and the sailors of the Newport sloop on St. Croix, Patricia Latreille arranged a few meetings between the colonists with eligible daughters and the sixteen sailors of the ship. She explained to these farmers and woodcutters that any man from this group would be a spectacular catch.

They were God fearing good men that she knew from her tavern. Most were from farming families and were unemployed sailors after the war. Working with Sam, they had been lucky and acquired small fortunes. Technically, they were all pirates but none of them viewed themselves as such and most of the ships they stopped for supplies while wrecking were partners in their larceny.

Only after they joined La Buse, when Sam was desperately in search of a ship suitable for becoming a man o' war, did they become real pirates. In June and July, they took two ships with La Buse but as soon as Sam took command of the Marianne and they reached St. Croix, the sailors of the Newport sloop stopped all acts of piracy and left the search for a new ship to Sam's new crew.

On a Sunday afternoon while Bellamy and La Buse were at sea, fifteen families with their twenty daughters aged thirteen to twenty showed up at Patty's Place to view these highly eligible bachelors who were rich, believed in God and came from farming families. Some of the farmers needed husbands for their aging daughters, some needed another able-bodied man around the farm and all of them needed more capital to grow their farms. Under the circumstances, it was only natural that the adults turned their heads and let nature run it's course among the lonely older men and the young girls looking for husbands.

Upon hearing the news that his original crew wanted to remain on St. Croix, Sam reacted with mixed feelings. This crew had worked well with him and he believed this was the safest life path for them to establish new lives and identities. The Africans and Miskito Coast Indians, with the exception of Gamba and John Julian, wanted to return to the Miskito Coast where they would feel welcome, especially after Captains Bellamy and La Buse left St. Croix. So, except for Gamba, John Julian, and Paulsgrave Williams, Sam was losing all the people he relied upon and truly trusted.

Captain James Martel

Chapter 12

Gambling on His Future!

Sam's biggest problem in preparing to leave St. Croix with the Sultana was that he had a hot-tempered crew prone to making irrational decisions and he could not always convince them to do things the right way. Still, Sam Bellamy and Paul Williams gave the men of the Newport sloop permission to stay in St. Croix.

Patricia insisted that the Captain's La Buse and Bellamy use their religious backgrounds to jointly marry all who wanted to get married and stay in St. Croix. This was particularly important to Patricia as she was hoping to get pregnant some day and didn't want a bastard child. They had already decided if it was a boy it would be named Thomas after Tommy, and if a girl, would be named Caitlin which was both an Old French and Irish name.

It was quite a ceremony as Sam dressed in his finest suit, which Tommy had made for him and La Buse was dressed in his robes from the Order of the Knights of Malta, which no one had ever seen or even knew he still possessed. As an ordained Priest, Captain La Buse read his prayers in Latin, which Sam was surprised to find he still understood. Sam read his portion in English from the Book of Common Prayer and no one showed concern that he wasn't an ordained minister.

One by one the married sailors and their wives left the party and the remaining sailors drank and danced until morning with an unusual camaraderie between the French and English Pirates.

It was agreed that the Marianne and the Newport

sloop would go to the Miskito Coast to pick up the newlyweds' share of the wrecking treasure. The sixteen married sailors wanted the treasure divided into seventeen shares so that all the newly married couples of St. Croix would start on an equal financial footing and there would be no conflicts because of money.

Sam agreed it was fair and consented. The two ships left the day after the wedding as Sam continued planning his return to New England. Tommy Tailor stayed behind and made 200 stout bags to carry the treasure on board the Sultana.

Sam was also hoping to leave John King behind with Patty and Tommy, but the crew and John King insisted he remain with the ship as they now had him trained as a "powder monkey" who had the dangerous job of replenishing powder to the guns in the middle of a battle. While Patty and Tommy knew it was wrong for a little boy to go to sea, they were frankly relieved, as the time spent with the pirates of the Marianne at Lynn's Laird did nothing to improve his temperament or manners.

Sometime after the first of the year, two pirate ships under the command of Captain Kennedy and Captain James Martel approached the Harbor and a cannon on the northeast entrance to the harbor fired a shot across their bow as an order to stand down. Kennedy and Martel demanded a parley and Bellamy and La Buse went out to meet with them.

As expected, by Bellamy and La Buse, Kennedy and Martel wanted access to the protected harbor to sell their trade goods to merchants and they wanted access to a beach to careen and repair their ships. With only a slight exaggeration, La Buse explained that there was only one suitable beach inside the harbor and that was still in use repairing, Bellamy's Sultana Galley.

They referred the Kennedy-Martel gang to Salt River where there was a splendid beach to careen a ship and the remnants of an old Flemish Fort to stop other ships from entering the Harbor. There were also protected roads to park ships out of sight to the east and west of the beach where the ships were being careened. Bellamy and La Buse promised to refer all merchant ships to Salt River Bay once Kennedy and Martel were set up in a defensive position.

They also had the Militia keep a close watch on the activity in the Salt River area as there was a network of trails and roads that had been in existence since the time of the Indians. This was another of those mysteries to Sam because none of these roads showed on the French maps in use at the time but the roads did allow Jean-Baptiste Labat to visit the colony around La Bassin after landing at Salt River. Also the network of roads is shown on the older Spanish Map. The roads had been crudely maintained by the British settlers who arrived after the French left.

None of the merchants or ships captains who reached La Bassin wanted anything to do with Martel unless in a fairly governed neutral port. Martel was almost as insanely cruel as Captain Vane and prone to holding hostages. Eventually, a London Merchant heard the story and reported to La Buse that La Bassin better be empty of the pirates he usually dealt with by mid month as he was compelled by honor to report Martel to the British Authorities for the looting and stripping of the King Solomon, a slave ship out of London. The King Solomon was owned by a Sephardic Jewish Merchant named Abraham Mendes and, at the

Memoirs of Captain Samuel Bellamy: 154

time, the Jewish Merchants of London stuck together.

Sam would leave St. Croix for what he thought was the last time to go to Blanco Island and recover the men left behind who he needed to man the Sultana Galley. He was concerned that he was unable to stay and help sort out the mess that he thought might develop from the presence of the Kennedy-Martel gang but hoped that the British Military would not risk provoking a major incident by invading the French Island of St. Croix.

Sam was cheered by his faith that the sixteen men from the Newport sloop could handle the situation. They were well armed, understood the paths and terrain around Salt River, and had the support of all the men of the island who had been trained to be part of the militia.

With regards to the crews of his ships, Sam had developed a plan to placate the most reluctant sailors and bring control to the rest of the crew. He was going to offer every sailor on the ship a full years pay (50 pounds sterling) for a few months journey to take his wrecking treasure from the Miskito Coast to the Coast of Maine where La Buse, Williams and Bellamy intended to set up a new pirate republic on one of the many hidden rivers along the coast. After they arrived, anyone who no longer wanted to be a pirate would still have their sailors pay, which Sam had promised and could make their way to Boston. Those who wanted to stay could remain with the pirate republic in Maine and prey on the rich ships off the New England Colonies and New France.

With these thoughts, Captain Sam Bellamy closed off the memories of his early life up to age 27. He carefully reviewed his manuscript so that he would name only those like Tommy Tailor and carpenter Thomas Davis who were not pirates. He verified that he had never named the 16 sailors from the Newport sloop nor the family names of their new spouses in his Memories. He then passed his memories to the person who was staying behind that he trusted the most and started the next chapter of his life.

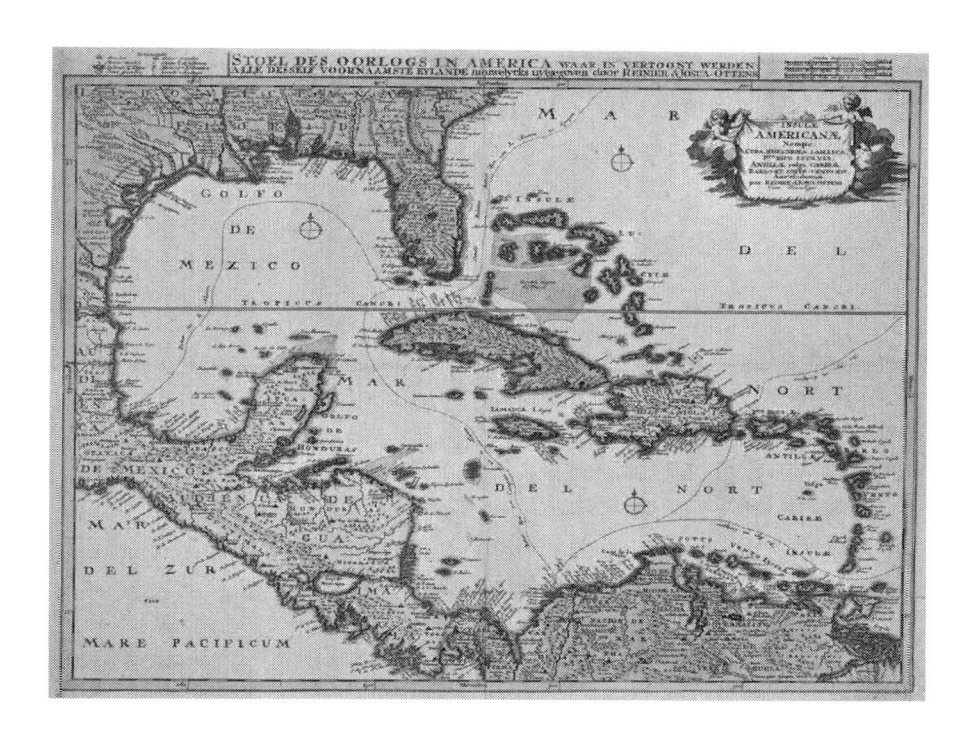

The Leghorn Map of 1715

Chapter 13

A New Ship for the New Adventure.

As Sam left St. Croix to start his new adventure, he was in excellent spirits. He was going to start a new pirate republic along the Coast of Maine and he was planning to reunite with Maria Hallett. All of the sailors willingly accepted Sam's offer. As pirates, they could not steal another pirates wealth regardless if one pirate wanted to save his wealth and the other spend. In most cases, they had to respect the Pirate Code's prohibition against stealing or be hung.

However if Sam wanted to give them a years worth of pay for a couple of months work then it was a gift from him and they could keep it. For the honest sailors and reluctant pirates, this was definitely honest pay for their participation in the dangerous work of moving a vast amount of wealth from the Miskito Coast to New England.

With Sam now Captain of the Sultana and Paul Williams elected as Captain of the Marianne, the crew elected Richard Noland to be the new Quartermaster for the fleet to replace Paul Williams. Noland's job was to do an accounting of Sam's wealth as they loaded it on ship and make sure that every sailor would get what Sam promised.

Noland was a favorite among the crew and trusted by everyone new and old. He was a gregarious Irishman and a seasoned sailor. He had not spent much time with the Royal Navy because he detested all things English. He gained his skill as an Irish fisherman in the North Atlantic, but as he grew older, he started sailing merchant ships because he liked the warmer climate of the Caribbean. He had been part of the crew of Captain Hornigold before joining forces with Sam and the rest of the pirates on the Marianne.

He made it perfectly clear to everyone he had no intention of returning to the cold waters of the North Atlantic and becoming part of the new pirate republic. He liked being a pirate and liked the Caribbean so his job would be to find a new ship on the way North and leave his accounting to the next quartermaster.

On the way to the Miskito Coast, the crew of the Sultana, both new and old, started working together as a team of seasoned sailors which most were. Sam kept Thomas Davis, the carpenter, close by as he was definitely the most reluctant and was actually hoping that they would encountered another ship with a carpenter so he would be let go.

As they sailed south to the Miskito Coast, they were lucky enough to cross paths with the Marianne and the Newport sloop. Sam warned Paul Williams that he should not stay in St. Croix but make a run for the windward passage between Haiti and Cuba to rendezvous with the Sultana for their trip North. He also told Paul to have the sailors of the Newport sloop remove their treasure to their individual farms as soon as they reached St. Croix and leave no evidence of piracy aboard the ship because the British might show up to do battle with Kennedy and Martel who had shown up after Captain Paul Williams had left.

The trip to the Miskito Coast was uneventful and Sam was greeted with a pleasant surprise. The Miskito Coast Indians wanted to be rid of all the wealth keeping only a share in copper coins and another in silver. When they had tried to trade gems or gold for items they needed, it raised so much interest and jealousy among the colonists and other tribes in the area that they were constantly being watched and under fear of attack.

When they gave some treasure away to the sailors from the Newport sloop, it stirred up more interest and they collectively decided that it was in their best interest to give it all away except for a small emergency stash that only the chief and Baba would know about. Once the tribe helped load the ship and tribe members told others that all the treasure was gone, they would be safer. Of course most members kept a few pieces as jewelry but could honestly say all the rest of the treasure was gone.

While the ship was being loaded, Sam reflected on the differences between sailing in the Caribbean and the North Atlantic during the winter months. In the Caribbean, the winds in winter were generally from the East or Northeast and only occasionally from other directions. The daily average wind speeds were generally steady with an average between 10 and 20 knots with gusts to 30 knots, which was fantastic sailing for larger sloops and galleys. On rare occasions, the wind would die off to a daily average of 3 knots, which meant the ships were very slow and difficult to maneuver giving the tactical advantage to his galley. Also, sea swells are usually around four to six feet while in the aftermath of a storm, the waves would be in the six to twelve foot range lasting from one day to a week. Winter months are relatively calm in the Caribbean compared to the summer hurricane season where sea conditions can be more difficult.

When going north from the Caribbean Sea to the open Atlantic Ocean, conditions dramatically change for the worse. Wind direction in winter is very erratic, changing from day to day and coming from any point on the compass. Average daily winds can range from

2 knots per hour to 33 knots per hour with gusts up to 70 knots. Sea swells in the Northern Atlantic are usually 10 to 15 feet in winter and even greater in storms. During a nor'easter in winter, waves at sea can be 40 to 50 feet high with rogue waves of even greater height. Still, Sam thought that the Marianne and the Sultana Galley were worthy ships with experienced crews that could safely manage the voyage.

Once fully loaded, the Sultana Galley made good time in heading towards the windward passage but the Marianne reached first. The crew of the Marianne had not yet heard of Sam's promise of pay to move a fortune to the Coast of Maine and create a new pirate republic, so they kept busy working the sea between Cuba and Hispaniola for provisions and whatever else of value they could find on the ships they stopped.

Once the two ships met, everyone agreed that there would be no more piracy until they were fully established in their new pirate stronghold in Maine. There was more than enough wealth to pay all the sailors on board with enough left over to fund their new stronghold. They had too much wealth to lose especially if they came to the attention of any of the naval powers of the Caribbean.

Shortly after they agreed upon the plan to be good, Sam spied the most spectacular frigate, which he knew he could convert into an unbeatable man o' war. The ship was a full rigged frigate with incredible speed approaching 13 knots. Sam wanted that ship and decided he would have it.

This frigate handled with high performance on all points of wind (i.e. going in any direction). Square rigs have twice the sail area per mast height compared to triangular sails, and when finely tuned at the hands of a master, they apply larger forces to the hull to move it faster. The result is that a full rigged ship can run down or away from a schooner of the same hull length.

The Sultana Galley was also fast at about 11 knots and the Marianne slightly slower. The frigate ran from them for three days while breaking for the more hostile environment of the North Atlantic. Fortune favored the hunter at the disadvantage of the prey and the winds died down in the vicinity of Long Island in the Bahamas where Sam caught up with the Frigate which fired a couple of shots from chase guns mounted in the bow of the ship.

A boarding party including Sam and Richard Noland proceeded to board the ship under a flag of parley. It seems that Captain Lawrence Prince knew the ways of pirates as he was an old man who claimed to have worked with Captain Morgan more than forty years earlier. He wanted the pirates to honor the pirate code and let him keep his ship even if they took all the commercial merchandise on board. *[According to the testimony of John Brown (a member of the crew who was hung in Boston), the cargo consisted of "Sugar, Indigo, Jesuits Bark [quinine] and some amount of silver and gold." This is widely quoted by historians prior to Barry Clifford claiming that the ship carried 4.5 tons of silver and gold.]*

Sam believed it was highly unlikely that this man was truly Lawrence Prince, the pirate, because that would make him almost 90 years old, which was unlikely for a pirate operating in the North Atlantic. If anything he believed he might be the son of Pirate Captain Prince who had never been a pirate and Sam wanted his ship. Still, he did not want to seem to violate the pirate code and take a ship from a pirate as that might give his own crew ideas and many of the pirates on the Sultana Galley wanted to believe that pirates could live to be ninety years old and beyond so they accepted the story on face value.

It was Richard Noland who stepped into this quagmire and resolved the dilemma. He negotiated between the two Captains and for his own benefit. Captain Prince agreed to relinquish his ship and 14 sailors (12 were volunteers) in exchange for Richard Noland and payment for the ship. He was well rewarded for his decision as he got to keep his own merchandise in addition to receiving the Sultana Galley and retaining from her "*as much of the best and finest goods as she could carry.*" *[According to John Brown, they gave Captain Prince "twenty pounds in silver and gold to bear his charges."]*

The crew loaded the cannons and the treasure from the Sultana Galley onto the frigate leaving behind the rich trade goods for Captain Prince. The fourteen new men stayed on the Frigate under guard. In the commotion of transferring the cannons and the treasure and keeping a guard on the new crew members, Noland jumped ship to stay with Prince on the Sultana Galley in the Caribbean.

[Note: Prince made it back to London in the Sultana. He continued sailing on a new ship called the Whidah and made two more successful voyages from London to Africa, across the Middle Passage to Jamaica and back to London. His final voyage was his most effective as he delivered 500 slaves to Jamaica while suffering only 3.3% loss of human life with no damage to the ship. Richard Noland lived long enough to get the King's Pardon under Governor Woods Rodgers and went to work for Captain Hornigold in Nassau after

Hornigold also got the Kings Pardon. Noland stayed on land as a prosperous man and Hornigold died at sea after he changed sides and became a pirate hunter working for Governor Woods Rodgers.]

Poseidon with Trident

Chapter 14

Poseidon's Revenge!

After the deal was agreed to Captain Prince became a most affable companion to Sam and Paul for the duration of their time together. He gave the history of the ship as best as he knew it and described the handling characteristics of the ship in rough seas.

According to Prince, The Whydah Gally was commissioned in 1715 in London, England by Sir Humphry Morice, a member of the British Parliament who inherited considerable wealth from his Father at an early age. As his business grew, he was considered the foremost London Slave Trader of his day. *[Note: It is hard to feel sorry for Sir Humphry Morice for the loss of his ship as he was simply not a nice person. Not only was he involved in the slave trade, but he used his position as a Governor of the Bank of England to embezzle funds from the Bank. He also embezzled from his own daughters' trust fund. When his financial empire started to collapse, he took the coward's way out and committed suicide.]*

Initially, Morice had sold his African captives to the Portuguese instead of incurring the risk of sending them across the Atlantic. When he decided to transport slaves to the Americas, he came to understand he would earn greater profits if the slaves were well fed with adequate water. He also used fast ships to make a shorter journey to insure fewer died in transit. Most ships also carried a ship's surgeon on the important Africa to Caribbean leg of the journey. Subsequently, the number of captives who died in Morice's ships on their journey to the American colonies was about half the average of his competitors. However, these were all profit driven decisions not humanitarian.

The Whydah Gally was a 300-ton, square-rigged three-masted frigate ship, 102 ft. in length and could travel at speeds up to 13 knots. Prince tried to explain to Sam that with a light load, the ship was very unstable in rough seas but Sam countered that he had been weaned on the HMS Bedford Galley in the North Atlantic during the War of Spanish Succession. Sam's comment brought up a discussion of the unusual name Whydah Gally for a ship that was a full sized frigate.

The ship had been christened the Whydah Gally as a threat to those who wished it harm. The Kingdom of Ouidah (pronounced WIH-dah) dealt in slaves with the Portuguese and Dutch. The Englishman, Morice, was a direct competitor to the kingdom in that he was willing to provide enslaved Africans to the other European slave Merchants regardless of their nationality.

At the time the ship was built, the word Gally had evolved from the word Gallows and meant "to frighten or to scare" and the name of the ship was a warning to the kingdom to be scared of the power of the ship. The Royal African Company first started naming ships with the use of the word Gally in 1700 and Humphry Morice commissioned his first two successful trans-Atlantic slave voyages in the Amey Gally under Captain Lawrence Prince (1710 &1711).

While Sam listened intently to the history of the ship, he showed disinterest in advice on how to sail it. He was not willing to concede that the Dutch were better sailors than the English so didn't pay attention to the advice of Captain Prince, the son of pirate Captain Prince. This Captain Prince was nearing sixty so Sam should have paid attention to the experience of a man who had survived twice Sam's age at sea in the North Atlantic and had learned to Captain a ship from his father. He would learn to listen to the wisdom of his elders in a short while and wish that he had paid more attention to the sage advise of Captain Lawrence Prince of the Whydah.

As Bellamy and Williams started sailing north from the Bahamas leaving Captain Prince behind in the Sultana, the sky became overcast and the wind from the west died down. The lookouts at the top of the mast saw the telltale sign of a major storm approaching as the horizon to the west first turned light gray and then a darker purple gray. As clouds, rain and sea engulfed the ship, they merged into an eerie foreboding gray color where it was difficult to see the front of the ship or distinguish a horizon that separated sea from sky.

The Marianne (sloop) dropped the foresail or jib and double reefed the main sail in preparing to put before the wind. Fortunately, the wind was coming from just North of West so it would take them away from the coast as they changed directions from their former northern course to one that would let them sail with the wind towards East by South and safely out to sea.

The storm hit the ships with a vengeance. The dark purple and gray front of the storm engulfed them and everything was gray as the waves rolled over the ship and the rains fell. The wind was so strong that the rain and sea spray blew sideways pelting and blinding the sailors. Lightening flashed and occasionally, one ship could see the other. Thus, lightening became both friend and foe. It allowed everyone to see that each ship was still afloat but they all were afraid that it would strike the ship splintering the mainmast with long shards of wood flying in every direction doing bodily harm or even knocking a sailor into a watery grave.

In preparation for the storm, Sam had made two critical mistakes, which almost cost him his ship. He treated the frigate as if it were a sloop. He took down all his small sails leaving the main sail, which meant he had more than twice the sail area in place, compared to the sloop. Also he had not changed course quickly enough so the wind and rain hit his boat from the side with the full mainsail up and almost turned over the ship. Fortunately, the force of the storm shredded his main sails and allowed him to put before the wind using the shredded sail to drive the ship.

Sam quickly learned his lesson and set two small foresails in a goose wing pattern (one to port, the other to starboard) to scud with the wind. Even this was too much sail and threatening to snap the mast so all sails were dropped and the Whydah brought her yards to port sailing only by the force of the wind on the mast and furled sails.

Controlling the ship became almost impossible in the swirling seas and Sam had the men set up blocks and tackle from the gun room to the tiller. It took four men in the gun room and two on deck to keep her head to the sea. If they failed and the ship were broached from the side, it surly would have rolled over and sunk. Steering the ship became especially important when a freak wave washed over the ship from bowspirit to poop deck washing the two sailors at the wheel overboard. They were lucky to be caught in the netting at the stern while the sailors on the gundeck held the ship on course.

The lightening continued all night long but was no

longer a friend. The sky was so dark that when lightening flashed, it temporarily blinded those looking at the sky and so they saw nothing. All the sailors on board huddled on the gun deck so they could quickly abandon ship without a thought that they had no place to go in this storm. As the storm raged on they had no friend except their ration of rum, which put them into a fitful sleep.

As the waves battered the wood ship, it began to make sudden sounds. Outside the wind howled in the rigging and loose chains on the slack side of the tiller began to rattle. As fear grew so did the rum fueled imagination of the sailors. They were sure that they heard the whispering of spirits walking around on the creaky wooden decks. Some claimed to see the ghosts of those who had been discarded overboard still wearing their chains which was where they thought the noise of rattling chains came from.

They continued scudding all night under their bare poles, but that was still too much force on their riggings. The next morning the main mast was at a skewed angle as it had sprung from the step and had to be cut away. The mizzen mast (rear mast) had also snapped and had to be removed.

During the day a few brave souls attempted to go on deck for fresh air but no one ventured to the lower deck (slave deck) or below to the hold. If they had they would have noticed the ship was starting to leak. As the storm from the mainland pushed the ships further out to the Atlantic, the warmer continental air began to interact with the winds from the North Atlantic. This created swirling seas and winds that came from every point on the compass. At first this made matters worst as the constantly changing storm front made control of the ship near impossible.

Eventually the wind from the North took control pushing the ship to the South.

The storm continued for three days and the sailors did the only thing they could; they prayed. About half the sailors were formerly Christian and invoked God for assistance to calm the storm, Jesus for redemption if the storm continued, and the Holy Spirit to protect them from the ghosts of enslaved Africans.

Sam was amused to find that the sailors who were hardened criminals had their own Trinity of sorts. They prayed to Hades to recall the ghost of enslaved Africans back to his domain so they could live in peace. They prayed to Poseidon, the "God of the Sea", to tame his domain and allow them to live. They also prayed to Poseidon's son, Proteus, the god of "elusive sea change" to calm the sea. Many also wanted Proteus to foretell their future with regard to survival and wealth, as he was capable of predicting the future. They knew Proteus was close as the sea was constantly changing. Those who feared the weather prayed to Zeus, king of the gods, the ruler of Mount Olympus and the god of the sky, weather, thunder, lightening and fate.

The wind and storm ended after four days and three nights and all the sailors claimed that it was their unique version of God that had saved the ship. Sam lost his temper over these petty arguments because if they failed to work together they would all be taking a one way trip to Hell regardless of what it was called or who ruled it.

The biggest problems they had to face were they were virtually dead in the water with only the foremast surviving and they had an excessive amount of water in the hold. They were even slower because they were riding so low in the water. Since there were only two tasks that were critical, Sam had all the available sailors man the pumps while Thomas Davis, with a few helpers, jury rigged new masts.

Captain Paul Williams was the first to recover sufficiently from the storm to bring the Marianne to the Whydah Gally so they could decide their new course of action. The sloop, Marianne, received no other damage than the loss of the main-sail, which the first flurry at the start of the storm tore away from the boom.

As Williams and Bellamy talked, progress was made on the Whydah Gally. The jury rigged sails allowed them to regain control and point the ship into the waves thus lifting the bow. As they emptied the water, they exposed a leak near the bow between two side planks. Thomas Davis soon had a temporary seal in the seam using tar coated hemp rope. It would have been better if sealed from the outside of the ship but he assured everyone that this would work as long as they didn't run into another storm like the last one.

Williams and Bellamy chatted with John Julian, the navigator, about where they were and where they should go. Sam knew he was no longer in charge of a floating fortress, a formidable "man o' war", but something closer to a derelict ship floating on the sea without control. If challenged by either pirates or military, he and his men would lose everything as they were unable to move quickly enough to be able to defend themselves. They briefly thought about trying for Rhode Island where they could be protected by Paulsgrave Williams' associates but decided it was too great a risk.

Upon reflection, they realized the storm had initially

carried them to the Southeast and the latter part of the storm driven by Northerly winds pushed them further south. While not exactly sure, they figured they might be in the vicinity of Hispaniola.

John Julian corrected them and told them they were further east because the first part of the storm was stronger and lasted longer. His instinct placed them North of the Virgin Islands and by heading South, they would have a fairly safe and quick sail to St. Croix. Once the crew was notified of their position and destination, the sailors all became jovial and the best of friends while planning for a raucous celebration of survival at Lynn's Laird.

As Sam returned to St. Croix, his spirits were lower than they had ever been in his life. All of his troubles started with the taking of the Whydah Gally, the beautiful full rigged frigate. The ship was a slaver and shortly after taking the ship many of his crew, including the Africans, came to believe the ship was haunted by the spirits of those who had died on the treacherous passage from Africa to the Caribbean. These spirits were on a mission to destroy the ship and punish all the sailors who had benefited from the profits of slavery including the pirates.

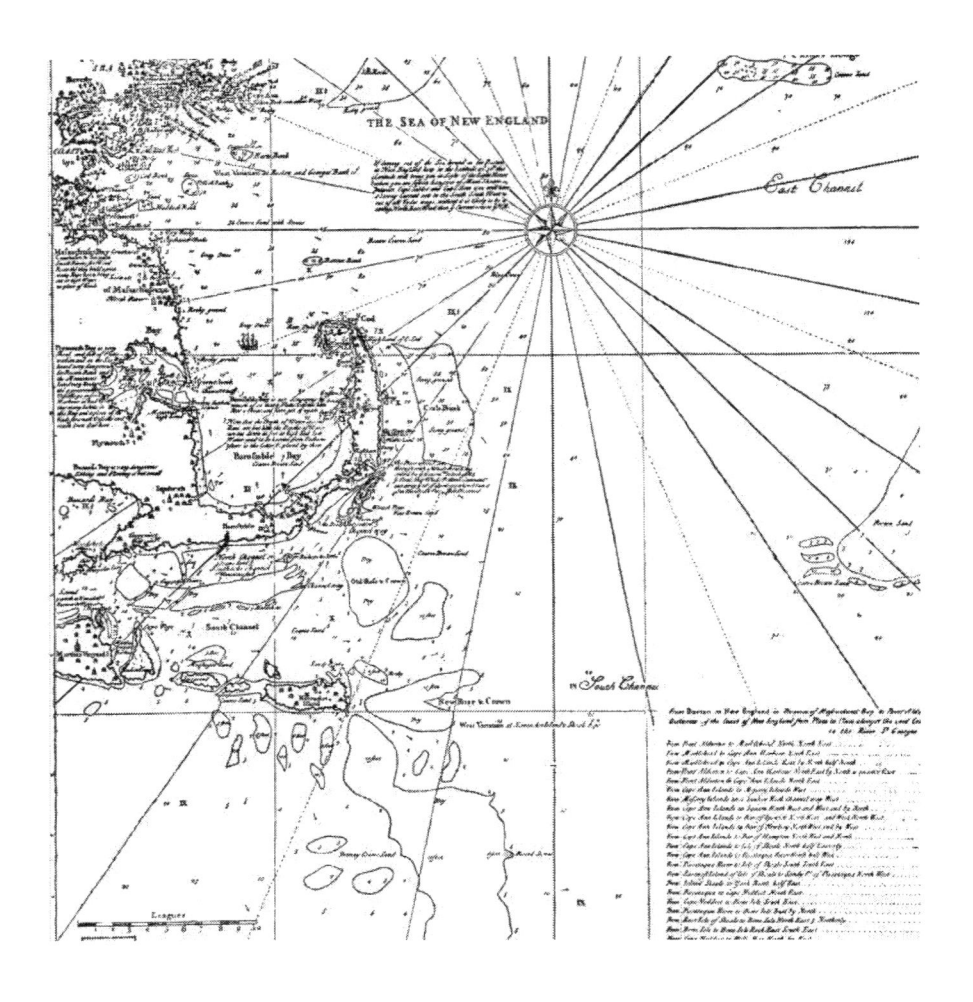

Cape Cod Map
of
Captain Cyprian Southack

Chapter 15
Final Reflections From St. Croix

When Sam got to St. Croix, he was too busy to concern himself with his memoirs. He knew instinctively that his first task should be to write about the taking of the Whydah Gally and almost sinking her in the storm. He had to reflect on his mistakes and learn to do better.

He made a new friend in Captain Adjett who was from a well-connected London Family. He was down on his luck and since the crew of the Newport sloop was busy being farmers they agreed to a partnership with Captain Samuel Adjett, which allowed him to use the Sloop in exchange for a share of the profits.

In the last war, Captain Adjett had been an officer on a small frigate and absolutely loved the small well armed war machines. After the war, he was financed by his family to become a merchant captain engaged in Caribbean trade. Between pirates and bad weather, he eventually lost his ship so he was glad to be alive, married and settled on St. Croix.

When he arrived about a month earlier, he had started a small warehouse operation in La Bassin where he met the sailors who were now farmers. They all knew that a small inter-island freighter running from St. Croix to neighboring islands could make money if combined with a warehouse so the profit could be made from both the savings in shipping and the retail profits. Adjett was happy to spend part of his time at sea and quickly learned the tricks of keeping a low profile and avoiding pirates. He was also not above buying supplies and trade goods from the pirates who still frequented the port. The farmers were happy to get lower prices while staying on land to work their farms.

Upon arriving, Tommy and Patricia Tailor met with Sam at her tavern and brought him up to date. The Martel/Kennedy-Martel gang did a terrible job of establishing a defensive position and used all of their cannons to defend their treasure in close proximity fighting. They had two cannons at the head of the road [anchorage] to the west of the peninsula where they were careening the ship. They had four guns guarding the treasure on this beach.

There were still eight guns on their original small sloop, which was in the middle of the bay also protecting the treasure on shore. The eight guns were rigged to fire hot grape shot, once again for close range fighting. When these guns were fired at the start of the battle, the grape shot went about 100 yards before falling harmlessly into the sea with little puffs of steam.

They had the other pirate ship of 22 guns in the west road behind the old Flemish Fort. The masts of the ship could be seen from the sea and fired upon, but the guns were worthless except for close in fighting because the fort blocked their ability to fire on a ship that stopped outside the reef. Initially, not a single gun was in position to fire on the HMS Scarborough anchored just outside the reef and Captain Hume started destroying the pirate ships at will. Depending on the wind and current, they came in close to fire at the ships and sink them or stood off until the weather improved before returning for more target practice.

After four days, the pirates tried to escape out of the harbor but were fired upon by Captain Hume's HMS Scarborough. Nineteen pirates, in a small sloop broke, out of the bay and left the vicinity. Captain Martel with forty pirates followed by twenty enslaved Africans ran up the west side of the bay towards the path to La Bassin. They were intercepted by the Island Militia, but not before the Africans had killed Captain Martel and a few of his sailors. The Africans and Pirates surrendered; the pirates because they were afraid of the Africans and the Africans because of the superior firepower of the Militia.

For the past month, the prisoners had been held under guard in two different locations because of the animosity of the two groups. They could have sold the Africans as slaves but none of the Island's planters wanted newly enslaved African that had to be broken and beaten into submission. The twenty Africans were being held in the slave pens behind Captain Adjett's warehouse and were well behaved considering the circumstances.

The thirty-five pirates who originally survived from the Martel gang were harder to understand. They constantly fought with each other. If a guard tried to break it up, they instantly united and attacked the guard. Subsequently, they were allowed to solve their own problems and were now killing each other at the rate of more than one per week so there were only twenty nine survivors left.

Sam went to the warehouse of Captain Adjett to see the enslaved Africans. Sam knew he would lose a few of his more superstitious sailors as a result of the storm and was in need of more good men. His current African sailors believed life as a free pirate at sea was better than being a black slave on a tropical plantation. He brought Gamba and a few of his African pirates along to act as translators.

Gamba took a leadership role in organizing the transition from enslaved Africans to free pirate. The Africans from the ship started teaching the prisoners English. The prisoners had to understand that on land and at sea they had to work for the good of the crew. They would get the same pay and the same amount of time off as all the other sailors working with Sam but they had to work for it.

In a couple of weeks, the crew was let free during the day to work on the ships and improve their English. These men were happy with their chance for freedom and were willing workers. The rest of the pirates appreciated their willingness to work and learn.

Now some of the pirates with Sam knew some of the pirates from the Kennedy/Martel Gang and thought they deserved the same chance as the enslaved Africans to regain their freedom. Sam agreed mostly, because he knew he needed more crew members (fighting marines) if he was to truly be Captain of a man o' war that would be the terror from Whydah.

Each man on Sam's crew was allowed to vouch for one man at a time if they chose. The man was expected to behave and obey the pirate code. Until they were trusted, they would be separated from the rest of their gang and take quarters in Captain Adjett's slave pen and seek no special privileges.

By the middle of March, all of the sailors and Africans had been assimilated into Sam's crew and the ship was well on its way to being repaired. During this period, Sam spent a lot of time with Captain Adjett learning the differences between sailing a full rigged frigate and a sloop or galley. He had definitely learned to respect the wisdom of his elders.

He now realized that sailing with a light load would mean he needed a lot more ballast. Fortunately, this was a problem with an easy solution as the Martel group had abandoned almost forty cannons at Salt River Bay with most on land or in shallow water.

Sam put Gamba and John Julian in charge of the salvage operation so they could recover the cannons for ballast. As a bonus, they recovered the silver that had been abandoned in the sunken ships during their hasty escape. Unlike ballast bricks, which were not available, cannons had to be lashed securely in place in the lowest part of the ship or they might break free and bounce around during rough seas potentially sinking the ship.

Meanwhile, Thomas Davis supervised the sailors in reconstructing the ship. In this safe Harbor, Bellamy would outfit the Whydah as a fortified transport to move his accumulated wealth back to the Boston area and set up his pirate republic in Maine. The men cleared the top deck of the pilot's cabin, removed the slave barricade, and got rid of other features that made the Whydah Gally top heavy. A small cabin for the captain, navigator and charts was at the stern with an exit to the gallery above the tiller. As cannons were recovered, they were secured in the hold as ballast. The goal was to make the ship more seaworthy in the expected rough seas of the North Atlantic.

Their new plan was to establish a base of operations on a hidden river along the coast of Maine. The Coast of Maine had been abandoned by the British after the last war so they could pick any place they liked without interference. All the pirates thought that the merchant ships would be richer prizes in New England and there would be fewer pirate ships competing with them.

Unfortunate, while dealing with his manpower problems, Sam came to understand that he had lost faith in his pirate republic and would rather have a small fortune and spend his life with Maria than to have all the money in the world in what he thought would be an irrational pirate republic. He came to understand that when there was a true democracy, people could be led astray and make very irrational decisions.

He still was not happy that the men had insisted that John King be allowed to leave his parents at age eight to become a pirate. He also was dwelling on the irrational behavior of the sailors of the Kennedy-Martel Gang while they were prisoners and had no faith that these men would make rational decisions in the long run. Even his own crew had failed him after the storm when they wanted to argue and fight about whose god had saved them rather than work together to save the Whydah Gally.

Since his run in with Jennings and Vane, Sam had tried to create a gang of honorable pirates who avoided violence and it seemed to work in small groups. But when good men abdicated, the fools ruled and so it was when he lost his original crew from the Newport sloop and became the Captain of the Marianne with Hornigold's crew.

Now, as he was preparing to go north, Gamba was going to retire to the Miskito coast with only a minimal share to bring with him because like Baba, Simba and Shumba he wanted no excessive wealth to cause conflict. Unlike the new Africans, he had seen the way that people from New England treated all Africans and he did not want to risk being captured again.

With a heavy heart, Sam called together Paul Williams, Gamba and John Julian and told them he was developing a plan to leave the ship and quit piracy. Gamba was relieved as he was planning on retiring to the Miskito Coast and now his conscience would be clear in leaving Sam. Paul Williams and John Julian decided they would stick together and continue to be pirates as it was still fun for them and they were not distracted by blind love for wives or girlfriends. His friends accepted his decision and cooperated with his plan for the future.

In the absence of Richard Noland, Paul Williams was both Captain of the Marianne and quartermaster for the fleet until the pirates could agree on a new quartermaster. The money that had been allocated for the sailors pay was separated and preserved in 200 bags contacting 50 pounds sterling for sailors pay with a little left over. These bags were secured between the decks of the Whydah and sailors were allowed to draw from their share.

Sam decided that he would leave an equivalent of two shares (twice the amount the sailors of the Newport sloop received) with his friend on St. Croix who was holding his manuscript and other personal items. This would be enough to establish a family on the island if he returned but not enough to cause jealousy among this group.

Sam's fortune was far larger as he still had all of his share of the pirate treasure accumulated since he became Captain of the Marianne and his share of the salvage treasure including the shares from the Miskito Coast Indians and the African divers who didn't want the money because of the problems it would cause.

Paul's fortune was equal to Sam's and he intended to

leave part of it with his family in Rhode Island while continuing to be a pirate. Greater wealth had never been a motivation for Paul becoming a pirate so he had no problem joining the rest of his fortune with Sam's to pay the crew and establish the pirate republic along the Coast of Maine. The extra silver on the Whydah, above the crew shares, was to establish the republic. Sam and Paul Williams combined their excess assets on the Marianne with Williams getting the best sailors from their combined crew.

They agreed that Paul would make arrangements to provide for his family and Maria Hallet, and that their combined treasure would be hidden safely on Block Island or in the nearby sea where they could legally recover it in a "wrecking operation."

Sam Bellamy knew that even as Captain, the pirates would not willingly let him retire, as they were too dependent on him. Unruly crews were just as likely to replace a captain and maroon the old one, as they would be to dispose of any other unruly sailor. The same was true of the carpenter, Thomas Davis, who had proved his value in saving the Whydah.

Because he had made the promise of freedom to Davis, he felt obligated to him just as Gamba had felt obligated to protect Sam so his plan had to include the both of them. When Sam talked with Thomas Davis, he explained how they both had the same problem even though Sam was Captain and Thomas was a prisoner. He also explained how, if they worked together, they both would be free men with enough money to start a new life.

Sam set the plan in action by alerting the crews to find enough barrels to store water for the month long trip to the Coast of Maine. Since he only had 140 men on board, he wanted all the below deck space filled with wood and water. The middle deck would store the food and any space left over would also be used for water barrels. On the gallery behind the Captains quarters, two barrels of water would be stored.

The only people going north that would know of the plan were Thomas Davis, the carpenter, John Julian, the navigator and Paul Williams, Sam's friend and quartermaster. The barrels on the gallery were specially fabricated by Davis to be like a Chinese puzzle with a smaller barrel firmly secured inside a larger one. Paul released gold and silver to Sam to fill the inner barrel. His interior barrel was filled with gold coins, the one for Thomas Davis was filled with silver. Both were filled less than their capacity to insure they would still float.

The gift for Thomas Davis was appropriate as he never willingly participated in generating the pirate wealth but was now being rewarded for the job Sam needed done. On the way north, Sam would teach John Julian the finesse of sailing a fully rigged ship so that when Thomas and Sam departed he would be at the helm and in control of the ship.

The plan was simple and relatively safe. When they got north of Boston, they would start searching for a bay where they would anchor to prey on smaller ships for supplies and whatever else they needed to create their permanent home. When they spotted a ship from the bay, the anchor would be abandoned and they would sail away in pursuit of the ship.

In the commotion of setting sail under the command of John Julian, Sam and Thomas Davis would push the barrels overboard and ride the surf to shore. The most dangerous part of the plan was to not freeze to death in the water before they reached land.

Once on land they would work their way south to Boston as traveling carpenters. Sam would call himself Thomas Hallot as he would instantly respond to the name "Hallett" and if somebody called Thomas, one of the two would respond. They would present themselves as impoverished carpenters whose only possessions were their wagon and tools which they would buy with silver as soon as possible. Thomas would keep both once they safely reached Cape Cod.

They would travel along the coast working for room and board where there was a shortage of men who had gone to sea but little money. Sam had done this on his way to Exeter and also when he worked his way from Boston to Newport and then back to Cape Cod. Their biggest task would be to not draw attention to themselves.

And so ends the Caribbean Memories

of

Captain Samuel Bellamy

St. Croix

March 24, 1717

The Diving Bell
of
Sir Edmond Halley
with
Compressed Air Reserves

Memoirs of Captain Samuel Bellamy: 185

Aftermath

After the Whydah Wreck.

The documented history of the Whydah wreck is more extensive than the history of Captain Sam Bellamy. This is because two trials were held for eight of the pirates who survived the sinking of the ship. Seven were tried in the first trial, with six being found guilty and sentenced to hang. Only Thomas South, who used a forced man defense, was found not guilty. He had been so nice to the three prisoners who also survived the storm that they testified on his behalf.

John Julian and Thomas Davis were the only known survivors from the Whydah, and Thomas Davis was tried in a separate case. Despite a confession of having sworn an oath of loyalty to all pirates, he was allegedly set free as a forced man or—as suggested by Cotton Mather—he received a pardon from the Governor for being cooperative and repentant.

Thomas Davis would have never been found to be a pirate if he had just walked away. It seems that he had lingered at the site for over four hours—more than enough time to stash some treasure, perhaps with help from John Julian. He then walked to the nearest house, which was occupied by Samuel Harding. He arrived at 5 am; the ship had sunk at midnight. A two mile walk for a healthy man should have taken way less than 45 minutes, so Davis would have had plenty of time to hide his stash.

Harding carried Davis back to the wreck on his horse and they had made several round trips between house and wreck to "*gett much riches*" according to Captain Cyprian Southack, the Governor's representative at the scene. Obviously, Davis was in very good shape and highly motivated, if they had managed to recover enough wealth to warrant several round trips between the wreck and Harding's house. Davis continued diving with up to 200 other wreckers for a few days more, until he was identified as a pirate and sent to the Boston Gaol. If he hadn't been tried for piracy, he should have been tried for stupidity.

John Julian, the free Black Indian from the Miskito Coast, was captured, and because he was Black, he was sold into slavery. He was an unruly slave, going through many masters. He was eventually hanged for killing a bounty hunter who was chasing him after he had escaped.

- Paulsgrave Williams survived the storm in Rhode Island. He allegedly received the King's Pardon, but reverted to a life of piracy off the African Coast, with La Buse as his partner.

- La Buse lived his entire adult life as a pirate, before finally being hung in 1730 after negotiations for a pardon broke down.

- A minimum of nine pirates from the Whydah survived the storm. Only 102 bodies were buried, and some of them could have been hostages captured the day before the Whydah sank. This leaves about fifty pirates not accounted for, but presumed drowned.

- The fragmented documents related to the trial from the Suffolk Court Files have no mention of the exact amount of wealth the Whydah contained.

- The report of the trial, printed by order of Governor Shute, also contains no mention of the exact wealth of the Whydah.

- The fragmented confessions of the pirates,

found in the documents from the Suffolk Court Files, are very different from those confessions printed by Governor Shute. These fragments do not mention the wealth of the Whydah.

- In the "substance" of the confessions printed by Governor Shute, the various pirates report different amounts of wealth. Some are imprecise, stating that there was a *"great amount of wealth on board"*; others gave precise answers of 180 bags with 50 pounds of silver and gold (4.5 tons). Other estimates ranged from 20,000 to 30,000 pounds (15 tons) of silver and gold.

- Any wealth recovered from a pirate ship in British territory belonged to the reigning Monarch, with a small portion awarded to those involved in the wrecking [recovery] operation.

- The Governor's report of the trial was not published until Cyprian Southack had secured the site and all the guilty pirates were hung. This was over a year after the Whydah had sunk.

- After securing the site, Captain Southack, a military man loyal to the King, wanted arrest warrants issued to detain and interrogate all those involved in the wrecking operation of the Whydah. His intent was to recover the King's gold and silver. Southack was an associate of Governor Shute, who had been appointed by King George; he was a friend of Sir Hovenden Walker, who had been politically connected to Queen Anne; and he had kissed the hand of King William.

- Governor Samuel Shute was also a military man loyal to king and country. He was a tenacious defender of what he believed was the King's property. In the Royal Forest of Maine, he blocked colonists from cutting any tree large enough to be used as a mast for a ship. This law reserving these trees for the King had largely been unenforced by previous governors because shipbuilding was an important industry in New England. Enforcement by Governor Shute led to political battles with the colonists.

- Cotton Mather was dogmatic, intractable, and a commiserate Whig. He has been described as the quintessential conservative Puritan leader. He shared a complete belief set with Governor Shute. He was an advisor to the Governor, and they were good friends.

- In the year after the sinking of the Whydah Gally, Cotton Mather preached several sermons on the dire spiritual consequences of "Getting riches and not by right," referring to the pirate treasure. The sermon was preached with reference to both the pirates and those people involved in the illegal wrecking of the Whydah and the taking of the King's treasure.

- Early in his career, Cotton Mather befriended William Phips, wrote his biography, and recommended to the King that Phips be made governor. In Phips's biography, Mather reports that Phips recovered 32 tons of silver from a Spanish wreck at a depth of 42 to 56 feet—a formidable task in any era.

- According to Mather, Phips discovered the location of the treasure, gathered what he needed for his expedition, and invented or adapted many of the tools he would need to recover the treasure. One of these tools was a diving bell that allowed men to work under water for a prolonged period.

- After Sir William Phips used a diving bell to bring his treasure to the surface in 1687, Sir Edmond Halley started designing a better bell in 1691.

- By 1716, Halley's bell would allow workers to stay under water for up to 4 hours. He also identified and solved the problems of compression and decompression sicknesses. Halley presented a paper in 1714 and conducted his experiments in the River Thames in London.

- Sir Edmond Halley was a friend and supporter of King George.

- Diving bells allowed divers to work in cold water for long periods, because the body does not lose heat as fast from 50 degree air in the bell as it would in contact with 50 degree water in the sea.

- Mather, Shute, and Southack would make an invincible team for recovery of the wealth of the Whydah from the inhabitants of Cape Cod, who had engaged in the initial wrecking operation on the Whydah. If Davis cooperated and identified those who recovered wealth from the wreck, then these three powerful men would be invincible, through their use of legal and moral pressure in recovering the King's treasure.

- The technology existed for recovery from a ship sunk in shallow water close to shore. Since the location of the wreck was known, and the equipment was available in London, Shute and Southack would be derelict in their duty to their King—and Mather would have been derelict in his duty to God—if the King's treasure aboard the Whydah was not recovered.

- In his book entitled "Cape Cod," Henry David Thoreau wrote: *"For many years after this shipwreck, a man of a very singular and frightful aspect used every spring and autumn to be seen traveling on the Cape, who was supposed to have been one of Bellamy's crew. The presumption is that he went to some place where money had been secreted by the pirates, to get such a supply as his exigencies required. When he died, many pieces of gold were found in a girdle, which he constantly wore."*

- More than two centuries later, Kenneth Kinkor, historian of the Whydah Museum, found a will for Mary Hallett of Yarmouth, whom he suspected was Maria Hallett. She had divided her substantial estate and bequeathed it to her family members with whom she was obviously reconciled. Her estate included silver spoons, gold rings, and a necklace of gold beads.

- There is no doubt that Barry Clifford discovered the wreck of the Whydah: The location is correct, the age of the artifacts is correct, and he may have discovered the ship's bell with the name on it.

- Barry Clifford recovered over 200,000 artifacts, ranging in size from a speck of gold dust to an 1,100 pound cannon.

- Conspicuously absent from the recovered artifacts are pistols, muskets, and precious metals. These are the same items that would have been valuable to the inhabitants and the King's representatives 300 years ago.

- The total amount of precious metals recovered was just 0.15 tons out of the 4.5 to 15 tons reported to be on board—or just 1 to 3 percent.

- After diving on the wreck for over thirty years, at a cost of almost $10 million, Barry Clifford found very little of monetary value. The only two conclusions that can be reached are:

    1. The methods and equipment used to locate the wreck of the Whydah, the ship's bell, 60

cannons, and over 200000 artifacts are amazingly inefficient at locating precious metals; or

2. The precious metals and personal weapons were recovered by the inhabitants and Captain Cyprian Southack about 300 years ago.

Year	1709	1710	1711	1712	1714	1715	1716	1718	1720	1721	1722
Captain	Lawrence Prince	Lawrence Prince	Lawrence Prince	Lawrence Prince	Lawrence Prince	Lawrence Prince	Lawrence Prince	Lawrence Prince	Lawrence Prince	John Dagge	John Dagg
Name	Amey Gally	Amey Gally	Amey Gally	Amey Gally	Whydaw	Whydah	**Whidaw Gally**	Whidah	Whidah	Whidah Gally	Whidah
Tons	150/272	150/272	150/272	150/272	200/305		300/343	250/365	250/365	310/354	300/343
City Built	London	London	London	London			London	London	London	London	London
Owner	Robert Heysham	Humpry Morice	Morice & Heysham				George Roberts ? ?	1717	Edward Dod 1717	Humpry Morice	Humpry Morice
Source	Africa	Bight of Benin	Africa	Africa		Bight of Benin	Whydah	Bight of Benin	Gold Coast	Gold Coast	Bight of Benin
Delivered	Jamaica	Jamaica	Jamaica	Jamaica	Jamaica		Jamaica	Jamaica	Jamaica	Jamaica	Jamacia
Slaves Wanted	550	550	500								
Slaves Loaded	550	340	604	562	624	367	367	460	517	273	357
Survived	437	290	550	450	500	313	313	420	500	236	304
% Loss	20.5	14.7	8.9	19.9	19.9	14.7	14.7	8.7	3.3	14.6	14.8
Notes				ship wreck, some slaves died on board		Voyage not complete natural hazard	Captured by Bellamy February 1717			Voyage ended, natural hazard Slaves transfered to other ship	Ship wrecked after delivery

Voyages of Captain Lawrence Prince 1709-1720
Trans-Atlantic Slave Trade Database
Emory University

Epilogue

Are the Memoirs True?

The Memoirs of Samuel Bellamy present a dramatically different impression from the current image of the man. His self-image is that of a wrecker and a businessman who stopped ships at sea out of necessity, and who occasionally became an accidental pirate. Even his own memoirs acknowledge acts of piracy, but not as a primary occupation. The only way this can be resolved is to return to the oldest original documents and read what they have to say.

The best record should have been from the trial of Bellamy's sailors who survived the storm, but the original trial transcript has been fragmented and portions lost. The first printed report of the trial was made under the guidance of a dogmatic governor who would have thought nothing of bending the law to support his King and perhaps recover a great fortune. The two versions do not always agree and are dramatically different on some major points. Authors and dates of publication for all sources are included in the **Annotated Bibliography** following this section.

Depending on the source, Sam was a pirate for two to fourteen months. By his own account, Sam admits being an occasional pirate for about 14 months. **JOHNSON (1728)** asserts that the taking of the "Whido" was Bellamy's first act of piracy, and that he was only a pirate for 2 months. Others estimate that Bellamy was active for about a year.

Another difference is that Bellamy described a very disorganized gang of pirates—men who were totally undisciplined and stopped every ship they saw, from fishing boats to merchant ships. They would linger and thoroughly loot every ship, instead of quickly moving on to the next prize. Contemporary sources suggest that Bellamy ran his ship with military precision, taking over 50 prizes during his career. In the testimony at trial, **JAMESON (1717/1923)** and **SHUTE (1718)** both describe a rather disorganized group of pirates, which is close to the description in Sam's Memoirs.

As to the number of ships taken, the testimony at trial and in Sam's Memoirs would seem to indicate the number is closer to 25 than to 50 and that many of those vessels were small fishing boats and other ships that were stopped for provisions. Regardless, Bellamy and Williams managed to gather a great amount of wealth.

There is not much historical debate about the vast amount of wealth the ship carried. Bellamy acknowledges 200 bags of silver weighing 50 pounds each, plus an undetermined amount of silver cogs for Thomas Davis and an equal amount for himself in gold coins. This would indicate a treasure of more than 5 tons. **JOHNSON (1728), JAMESON (1717/1923),** and **MATHER (1717)** make no specific mention of the vast wealth of the Whydah. The greatest focus on the specific wealth of the ship is in the report authorized by Governor Shute **[SHUTE (1718)]**. Some confessions describe it as vast wealth, but those pirates who describe a specific amount claim from 180 50-pound bags of silver (4.5 tons) up to 30,000 pounds of silver and gold (15 tons). Overall, a minimum estimate of 5 tons of silver, with a small amount of gold, seems very reasonable. This is consistent with Barry Clifford's original estimate of 4.5 tons. Clifford also reported finding 660 times more silver than gold by ounces recovered, which is consistent with Bellamy's claim of loading mostly silver onto the ship.

The biggest difference in all the versions is the source of the wealth. None of those who were tried for piracy mentioned the capture of any great prizes. Of course, none of those captured was part of the original wrecking crew. Even the capture of the Whydah describes the exchange of ships as a business transaction. Both records of the trial, **JAMESON (1717/1923)** and **SHUTE (1718),** are consistent in their descriptions of the transaction. When captured, the ship was laden with sugar, indigo, Jesuit's bark (quinine), and some silver and gold. In exchange for his ship, Captain Prince was given the Sultana, which was loaded with as much of the best and finest goods as she could carry. Bellamy gave Captain Prince an additional twenty pounds in silver and gold to cover his costs. As discussed below, returning to London with bulky trade goods of limited value to pirates would have been consistent with the businesses practices of Humphry Morice and other ship owners.

While the historic record is not entirely clear, Captain Lawrence Prince worked for Humphry Morice starting in 1710. According to **RAWLEY (1718-1731/2003)**, Morice was a very detail-oriented manager who worked closely with his captains and rewarded them with profit sharing and personal loyalty. His method to earn a profit was direct. He took trade goods to Africa from England and Holland. When the ship arrived in Africa, the captain would consult with the captains of other ships in the area to maximize the utilization of his ship.

The first objective was to convert all the trade goods into gold and silver, which would be consolidated in one ship. That ship would then return to London, together with any other desirable trade goods, like elephant teeth (ivory). If his trade goods could only be traded for slaves, the slaves should be sold in Africa for gold and silver and would follow the usual path of bilateral African-English trade.

Only under unusual circumstances would a captain take the dangerous and deadly mid-Atlantic passage. The objective was to consolidate the slaves from all his ships, dispose of excess African slaves in Barbados or Jamaica, and return to Africa with rum for trading. As an alternative, the captain might pick up sugar, tobacco, or lumber in the colonies and return to London.

In this manner, his ships avoided carrying anything that pirates might want, and his fleet was relatively free from pirate attacks. At no point would a captain remain in port for more than 3 weeks. It was better to return empty and start another voyage without wasting time. Unfortunately for Captain Prince, Captain Bellamy was not interested in trade goods. He wanted the ship itself.

At all times, Morice had multiple ships at sea and focused his trading activities on the African coast, in the vicinity of the Bight of Benin. His captains were trained to talk with each other and make decisions on their own, within his general guidelines, or minimally, in his best interest. Records of the voyages of Captain Prince, **VOYAGES (1514-1866/2008)**, do not even suggest a blight on his relationship with the London slave-traders caused by the loss of the Whydah.

Lawrence Prince started his career as a captain of slave ships in 1700, working for various investment groups. He made five voyages with various groups of owners, and on his fifth voyage, he only lost 8.9% of his enslaved Africans due to sickness. Most other captains were losing more than 20%. He then captained a ship owned by Robert Heysham, one of the wealthiest London slave-traders and English politicians. His first trip on the Amey Gally was average, experiencing a 21% loss in human lives. Ownership of the same ship was next reported to be Humphry Morice, who was known to be very active in training his captains and remaining loyal to them. On this voyage, losses were 14.7%. The final voyage with named owners indicated a partnership of Morice and Heysham and losses continued to decline, to 8.9%.

On Prince's final voyage on the Amey Gally in 1712, the owner is not noted. Prince's ship succumbed to natural causes at sea, and his loss of enslaved Africans rose to 19.9%. This was his last documented voyage on a ship previously owned by Humphry Morice.

Prince's next two voyages were for unspecified owners, on ships named Whydaw and Whydah. One of the difficulties with tracking records in the early eighteenth century was the very careless spellings that were tolerated, and even accepted, in official records. The two trips were in 1714 and 1715, and the second ship also never completed its intended voyage due to natural causes.

Prince's voyage of 1716 was in the infamous "Whydah Gally," and the documentation in the Slave Trade Database is uninspiring. The ship's owner, George Roberts, seems to be either a lowly seaman or a fictitious character from a Defoe book. Most 18th century owners of slave ships are easy to document because they had to be independently wealthy and engaged in international trade to enter into slave trading.

These owners also seem to have invested in many different ships, as did Edward Dod, owner of Captain Prince's last ship, the Whidah, which he used for voyages in 1718 and 1720. Other than the single entry for the Whidaw Gally, Roberts does not show up again until 1738, when he appears as a partial owner of another ship.

It would appear that Captain Prince was not always truthful in his discussions with Sam Bellamy. Not only was he not a pirate, he was no longer working for the richest and most powerful London slave trader of that era, Humphry Morice.

The record from the Slave-Trade Database shows the proper name of the ship as the Whidaw Gally, with the spelling unlike any other ship under Captain Prince's command with a similar name.

William Snelgrave is responsible for documenting the name the Whidaw Galley. In his book, **Snelgrave (1734)** describes being captured and detained by pirates off the Coast of Africa, including Paulsgrave Williams and Oliver La Buse. In 1719, both captains were down on their luck, having lost the ships they had sailed in 1717. They were operating together on a ship, with the worst sort of gangsters as their crew. They had been elected as Quartermaster and Captain, but they were definitely not the owners of the ship and served at the whim of a very unruly, irrational crew.

Snelgrave describes Williams as the *"Commander of a pirate sloop; who with a brigantine, two years before, took Captain Lawrence Prince in the Whidaw Galley near Jamaica."* Since Captain Snelgrave knew Captain Prince, and in his book, he confirms Williams as one of the Captains involved in the piracy of his ship, this spelling will be assumed to be correct by historians until such time as the bell discovered by Barry Clifford is independently and scientifically authenticated.

Sam's diary is consistent with the name used by the pirates at the Boston trials. He calls the ship the Whido, which was definitely not the original name of the vessel. Whido does not show up in any of the historical records, unless connected to the pirate ship after it was acquired from Captain Prince.

To further confuse matters, Humphry Morice launched two more ships under the command of Captain John Dagg(e), named the Whidah Gally and the Whidah. You can see in the Table at the start of this chapter that those two ships are different, simply by looking at the tonnage of the vessel calculated by two different methods. Both ships were wrecked due to natural causes.

Captain Dagge was captain for three more voyages on ships owned by Humphry Morice, despite losing two ships in a row to natural causes. The second Whidah, captained by Dagge, appears to have been built to the same tonnage specifications as the Whidaw Galley that Captain Prince traded to Captain Sam Bellamy.

A final anomaly in the data is that the voyage of the Whydah in 1715 started with exactly 367 slaves, as did the Whidaw Gally in 1716, despite differences in the availability of slaves at the Bight of Benin or differences in each ship's capacity. Both voyages ended with exactly 313 slaves, despite differences in sailing time and variations expected from the percentage lost to disease. As an engineer, I always double check the accuracy of data that is exactly the same, especially when the outcome is influenced by random variations in natural phenomena.

In the end, it is the ship's bell that is all important in correcting the name in the historical records, just as the ship's bell was all important in creating the future for a young Barry Clifford.

Without the Whydah Gally bell, it is doubtful that the Massachusetts Board of Underwater Archaeological Resources would have granted Clifford a permit to secure the site for his exclusive exploration. Since he could not have secured the site without the bell, he would not have been able to secure financing when E. F. Hutton sold stock in 1987, in a limited partnership, which financially supported the continued excavation of the Whydah Gally site.

Personally, I don't doubt that Barry Clifford discovered the pirate ship of Captain Sam Bellamy. The ratio of silver to gold matches the Memoirs of Captain Sam Bellamy in loading the ship. The need for the massive number of cannons stored in the hold as ballast also matches the Memoirs of Captain Sam Bellamy.

However, until such time as the bell is independently authenticated, there is not much to convince me that it is authentic, or that Emory University should alter the records in the Trans-Atlantic Slave Trade Database.

Annotated Bibliography

JAMESON (1717/1923) Two different, and somewhat conflicting, transcripts describe the testimony about life on the Whydah. The most accurate should have been the one compiled from the Suffolk Court Files. Most of the documents in the file are highly fragmented, many parts are missing, and the part that remains was not published until 1923. Also included as part of the knowledge of the sinking of the Whydah are two letters from Cyprian Southack to Governor Samuel Shute, written during the first part of May, 1717 (May 5th and May 8th), describing his findings. This book is titled:

> PRIVATEERING AND PIRACY IN THE COLONIAL PERIOD
> EDITED UNDER THE AUSPICES OF
> THE NATIONAL SOCIETY OF THE
> COLONIAL DAMES OF AMERICA
> BY
> JOHN FRANKLIN JAMESON
> DIRECTOR OF THE DEPARTMENT OF HISTORICAL
> RESEARCH IN
> THE CARNEGIE INSTITUTION OF WASHINGTON

This exceptional volume is available online as part of the Gutenberg Project. It can be accessed online at www.gutenberg.org. For pirate buffs or historians, it is well worth reading in its entirety. The discussion of "The Pirates of the **Whidah**" starts with the first letter from Southack to the Governor and is document 107. In the text, the ship is referred to as the **Whido**.

MATHER (1717) Cotton Mather's pamphlet, "*Instructions to the Living; from the condition of the Dead*" (Boston, 1717), is still available online. It has been preserved in the Evans Early American Imprint

Collection at the University of Michigan. However, other than being a pamphlet on a timely topic of interest to the people of Boston, it contains no details of piracy or the wealth of the Whydah. Mather uses **Whido, Whida**, and **Whidau** for the name of the ship.

SHUTE (1718) The complete trial transcript, plus a little more, was published by Governor Samuel Shute on May 22, 1718. The book is entitled "*The Trials of eight persons indicted for piracy etc. Of whom two were acquitted, and the rest found guilty.*" A very excellent electronic version is available online through the Evans Collection at the University of Michigan. The book also includes an Appendix with the "substance" of the alleged confessions of the pirates. The ship is consistently called the **Whido.**

RAWLEY (1718-1731/2003) "*London, Metropolis of the Slave Trade,*" by James A. Rawley, 2003. Chapter 3 contains a detailed description of the business practices used by Humphry Morice in his slave-trade between 1718 and 1731. Morice's records still exist and are held and archived by the Bank of England. The Whydah Gally is not mentioned.

JOHNSON (1728) "*A General History of the Pyrates,*" was published in 1724, with only a cursory mention of Bellamy with a first name of Charles. That is hardly an acknowledgment of the wealthiest pirate of the Golden Era.

Volume II, published in 1728, mentions three fictitious prates, and a fair number of political diatribes and flights of fancy. The complete edition of Volume II is difficult to find perhaps because it is so poorly written. Volume I has never been out of print since its original publication date and is available in many different versions. In the difficult to find or enjoy Volume II, Sam Bellamy rated Chapter XIII.

I finally found Volume II in a Kindle edition, edited by Manuel Schonhorn, who attributes the authorship to Daniel Defoe. This edition of *"A General History of the Pyrates"* was published by Dover Maritime and offered in the Kindle Edition by Dover Publications.

In 1972, before Barry Clifford had discovered the wealth of the Whydah, Schonhorn went on record stating that so few facts are present in Defoe's account of Bellamy that his information might or might not have come from newspapers of the time. Also, there are so few similarities of information and phrasing that it is not possible to argue convincingly that Defoe used newspapers or any other public source for his information on Bellamy. The only thing in Defoe's writing that appears certain is that he thought the taking of the **"Whido,"** in February 1717, was Captain Samuel Bellamy's first and perhaps greatest act of piracy.

Snelgrave (1734) "A new account of some parts of Guinea etc." While this book was published in 1734, after Humphry Morice died, William Snelgrave states that he wrote the account of his being captured by a group of pirates, including La Buse and Williams, immediately after he returned to London, in 1720. In his book, he is extremely complimentary of the humanitarian business practices of Humphry Morice and equally disdainful of the irrational, drunken, and mean-spirited actions of the pirates. He seems to like Captains Davis, Williams, and La Buse, while apparently was not fond of Captain Cocklyn. His account of his interactions with the various pirates is one of the most believable I have ever read.

While the book is a quick and fairly easy read, it is not for the weak of heart. It is written from a perspective of white British supremacy and is totally lacking in cultural sensitivity for other European cultures, in general, and Africans, in particular. This is the first reference I find where the ship's name is **Whidaw,** and this citation is probably the source for the name used in the Trans-Atlantic Slave Trade Database. He confirms the date the ship was taken.

Strong (1836) *"The Lives and Bloody Exploits of the Most Noted Pirates, Their Trials and Executions, Including Correct Accounts"* by Ezra Strong. This account is purely plagiarism of Volume II produced by Captain Johnson. It is easier to read because spelling and grammar rules are much closer to current usage. This is the next reference I find where the ship's name is **Whidaw,** which is consistent with Snelgrave and the Trans-Atlantic Slave Trade Database.

COOPER (1856) *"History of the Navy of the United States Of America"*, By J. Fenimore Cooper. Continued To 1856. Authorized by an Act of Congress, in the year 1853. Cooper describes the sinking of a ship named **Whidah** off Cape Cod in 1717. Available on line at:
http://www.archive.org/stream/histnavyusa00coopric h/histnavyusa00cooprich_djvu.txt

VOYAGES (1514-1866/2008) *"Trans-Atlantic Slave Trade Database"* by Emory University. This is a fascinating registry of ships, captains, owners, and slaves transported, including all available data and information. In this registry, the ship is called **Whidaw Gally.** Available on line at:

http://slavevoyages.org/tast/database/search.faces

Vox audita perit, littera scripta manet.

Final Thoughts on the Words of William Snelgrave

Throughout this book, I chose to use the name Whydah Gally, as spelling in general was very bad and inconsistent at the start of the eighteenth century. In defense of William Snelgrave, he is an excellent writer.

While he uses the punctuation and capitalization rules of his era, his spelling is consistent. He wrote the Whidaw Nation, the Whidaw King, the Whidaw people, the fort at Whidaw, so the ship of Captain Prince, according to Snelgrave, was the Whidaw Galley.

There can be no doubt that Gally and Galley are two different words, Gally means to fear and is derived from the word Gallows. It first came into usage around 1695. The period from 1700 to 1735 covers the era of all of the captains in this book engaged in the slave trade or who took possession of slave ships. During this period, the *Trans-Atlantic Slave Trade Database* documents 459 voyages with ships that include Gally or Galley in their name. Of these, ninety percent (90%) used the word Gally, by far the more popular choice.

In fact, none of these ships were actually galleys in the traditional sense. Using men on oars is a horribly inefficient and a slow method of transportation. A galley would travel at less than half the speed of a square rigged ship. To row a ship of this size, even at the slower speed, would take almost 150 men continuously manning oars. Also, a slave manning the oars burns three times the calories as a sedentary man. This would increase costs or the slaves would arrive in very poor condition.

The ships owned by Humphry Morice had a relatively small crew of fewer than 50 sailors, who would transport between 350 and 650 enslaved Africans, with two thirds being healthy men.

The captains were instructed to take care of the slaves and not abuse or allow damage to them. The slaves were to be well fed, be given regular baths, and receive adequate medical care. There was a Free African linguist on board, along with a ship's surgeon. It was the job of the linguist to make the needs of the enslaved known to the Captain and the ship's surgeon. The use of "galley-built" ships by Morice was also consistent with the need to keep the enslaved Africans alive, to maximize profits.

According to Captain Snelgrave, a galley-built ship was unique in that there were only two flush decks above the hold. The lower deck was divided into three main sections. At the stern of the ship was the gunpowder room. This could only be accessed from the great room under the quarterdeck. It was sealed off from the slave area by a bulkhead. The next quarter of this deck was the area where the women and children were locked down, and the front half of this deck was the confined area for chained men.

This configuration carried about half the number of slaves as a ship with four or five flush decks with limited headroom, so the initial cost for slaves was about half. Since a much greater percentage of enslaved Africans reached America alive, profits for the voyage were equal or greater for the ships of Humphry Morice.

My choice of calling the ship the Whydah Gally gives Barry Clifford the benefit of the doubt over very inconsistent 18th century spelling. I would feel far more comfortable with this decision if the bell was authenticated by independent experts.

Printed in Great Britain
by Amazon